Contents

- What is Java 1
- Java Example 1
- Application 1
- Types of Java Applications 2
- Java Platforms / Editions 2
- History of Java 3
  - Why Java named "Oak"? 4
  - Why Java Programming named "Java"? 4
    - Java Version History 5
- Difference between JDK, JRE, and JVM 5
  - JVM 5
  - JRE 6
  - JDK 6
    1. Java 9 REPL (JShell) 8
    2. Factory Methods for Immutable List, Set, Map and Map.Entry 8
    3. Private methods in Interfaces 9
    4. Java 9 Module System 10
    5. Process API Improvements 10
    6. Try With Resources Improvement 11
    7. CompletableFuture API Improvements 12
    8. Reactive Streams 12
    9. Diamond Operator for Anonymous Inner Class 12
    10. Optional Class Improvements 13
    11. Stream API Improvements 13
    12. Enhanced @Deprecated annotation 14
    13. HTTP 2 Client 14
    14. Multi-Resolution Image API 15
    15. Miscellaneous Java 9 Features 15
  - Java 9 Reactive Streams 16
  - Java 9 Flow API 17
  - Java 9 Flow API Classes and Interfaces 18

Java 9 Reactive Stream Example 19
Stream Data 19
Subscriber 20
Reactive Stream Test Program 21
Message Transformation Example 23
Processor 24
Message Transformation Test 26
Cancel Subscription 27
Back Pressure 28
Introduction 28
Hot and cold Observables, and multicasted Observables 28
Useful operators that avoid the need for backpressure 29
Throttling 29
sample (or throttleLast) 30
throttleFirst 30
debounce (or throttleWithTimeout) 30
Buffers and windows 31
buffer 31
window 33
Callstack blocking as a flow-control alternative to backpressure 35
How a subscriber establishes "reactive pull" backpressure 35
Reactive pull backpressure isn't magic 36
Implementing custom operators (draft) 38
Introduction 38
Considerations 39
Observable protocol 39
Unsubscription 39
Backpressure 40
Concurrency 41
RxJava tools 41
The queue-drain approach 42
Creating source operators 44

Converting a callback-API to reactive 45
Creating intermediate operators 46
Java 9 features with examples 48
- 1. Improved Javadoc 49
- 2. Factory methods for collections(like List, Map, Set and Map.Entry): 49
- 3. JShell: the interactive Java REPL 50
- 4. Stream API Improvements: 50
- 5. Private methods in Interfaces: 51
- 6. Multi-Resolution Image API: 51
- 7. The Java(9) Platform module system: 51
- 8. Improvements in Process API: 52
- 9. HTTP/2 Client 52
- 10. Miscellaneous Java 9 Features: 52

What is new in Java 9? 54
Process API updates in Java 9 54
HTTP/2 client in Java 9 54
Trending Courses in this category 55
4 (10900) 56
28k Learners Enrolled Live Class 56
Best Price **16,995** ~~19,995~~ 56
Similar CoursesSpring Framework Certification TrainingComprehensive Java Course Certification TrainingPython Scripting Certification Training 56
Java Shell Scripting (Read-Eval-Print-Loop) in Java 9 56
Multi-release JAR files feature in Java 9 56
More Concurrency Updates feature in Java 9 58
Project Jigsaw in Java 9 58
So, this was all about Java 9 and new Java 9 features. 60

Java 10 is finally here! A closer look at the new features 61
Java 10 is final – Is it that time again? 62
Java 10 – The new features 62
Long Term Support Model 67
Oracle JDK vs Open JDK 68
Java 10 Features 68
- 1. Time-Based Release Versioning (JEP 322) 69

2. Local-Variable Type Inference (JEP 286) 70
3. Experimental Java-Based JIT Compiler (JEP 317) 70
4. Application Class-Data Sharing (JEP 310) 71
5. Parallel Full GC for G1 (JEP 307) 72
6. Garbage-Collector Interface (JEP 304) 72
7. Additional Unicode Language-Tag Extensions (JEP 314) 72
8. Root Certificates (JEP 319) 73
9. Thread-Local Handshakes (JEP 312) 73
10. Heap Allocation on Alternative Memory Devices (JEP 316) 73
11. Remove the Native-Header Generation Tool – javah (JEP 313) 74
12. Consolidate the JDK Forest into a Single Repository (JEP 296) 74
13. API Changes 74

Java 10: New Features And Enhancements 76
  Let's take a sneak peek into what new features are in Java 10. 76
  Removed Features and Options in Java 10 78
  Deprecated Features and Options in Java 10 80

Why is Java 11 important? 83
Which JDK build should I download and what are the benefits of each of them? 83
How to download Java 11 Free Version? 84
Java 11 Features 84
  Running Java File with single command 84
  Java String Methods 85
  Local-Variable Syntax for Lambda Parameters 87
  Nested Based Access Control 87
  JEP 309: Dynamic Class-File Constants 88
  JEP 318: Epsilon: A No-Op Garbage Collector 88
  JEP 320: Remove the Java EE and CORBA Modules 89
  JEP 328: Flight Recorder 89
  JEP 321: HTTP Client 89
  Reading/Writing Strings to and from the Files 89
  JEP 329: ChaCha20 and Poly1305 Cryptographic Algorithms 90
  JEP 315: Improve Aarch64 Intrinsics 90
  JEP 333: ZGC: A Scalable Low-Latency Garbage Collector (Experimental) 90
  JEP 335: Deprecate the Nashorn JavaScript Engine 90

90 New Features (and APIs) in JDK 11

Developer Visible Features

JEP 323: Local-Variable Syntax for Lambda Parameters
JEP 330: Launch Single-File Source-Code Programs
JEP 321: HTTP Client (Standard)
JEP 320: Remove The Java EE and CORBA Modules

New APIs

Non-Developer Features

JEP 181: Nest-Based Access Control
JEP 309: Dynamic Class-File Constants
JEP 315: Improve Aarch64 Intrinsics
JEP 318: The Epsilon Garbage Collector
JEP 324: Key Agreement with Curve25519 and Curve448
JEP 327: Unicode 10
JEP 328: Flight Recorder
JEP 329: ChaCha20 and Poly1305 Cryptographic Algorithms
JEP 331: Low-overhead Heap Profiling
JEP 332: Transport Layer Security (TLS) 1.3
JEP 333: ZGC A Scalable, Low Latency Garbage Collector
JEP 335: Deprecate the Nashorn Scripting Engine
JEP 336: Deprecate the Pack200 Tools and APIs

Shorter Version

The Longer Version

Introduction

The New Six Month Release Cadence and LTS

Oracle Updates Plan

OpenJDK Updates Plan

Java SE / OpenJDK Providers

Why Would I Choose Commercial Support?

Provider Summary

Linux Distros

AdoptOpenJDK

Azul 116

IBM 117

Oracle 117

Red Hat 118

Java Desktop / Java Web Start / JavaFX 119

FAQ 121

Conclusion: 124

What is Java

Java is a **programming language** and a **platform**.

Java is a high level, robust, object-oriented and secure programming language.

Platform: Any hardware or software environment in which a program runs, is known as a platform. Since Java has a runtime environment (JRE) and API, it is called a platform.

Java Example

Let's have a quick look at Java programming example. A detailed description of hello Java example is available in next page.

1. **class** Simple{

2.   **public static void** main(String args[]){
3.   System.out.println("Hello Java");
4.   }
5. }

Application

According to Sun, 3 billion devices run Java. There are many devices where Java is currently used. Some of them are as follows:

1. Desktop Applications such as acrobat reader, media player, antivirus, etc.
2. Web Applications such as irctc.co.in, javatpoint.com, etc.
3. Enterprise Applications such as banking applications.
4. Mobile
5. Embedded System
6. Smart Card
7. Robotics
8. Games, etc.

Types of Java Applications

There are mainly 4 types of applications that can be created using Java programming:

1) Standalone Application

Standalone applications are also known as desktop applications or window-based applications. These are traditional software that we need to install on every machine. Examples of standalone application are Media player, antivirus, etc. AWT and Swing are used in Java for creating standalone applications.

2) Web Application

An application that runs on the server side and creates a dynamic page is called a web application. Currently, Servlet, JSP, Struts, Spring, Hibernate, JSF, etc. technologies are used for creating web applications in Java.

3) Enterprise Application

An application that is distributed in nature, such as banking applications, etc. is called enterprise application. It has advantages of the high-level security, load balancing, and clustering. In Java, EJB is used for creating enterprise applications.

4) Mobile Application

An application which is created for mobile devices is called a mobile application. Currently, Android and Java ME are used for creating mobile applications.

Java Platforms / Editions

There are 4 platforms or editions of Java:

1) Java SE (Java Standard Edition)

It is a Java programming platform. It includes Java programming APIs such as java.lang, java.io, java.net, java.util, java.sql, java.math etc. It includes core topics like OOPs, String, Regex, Exception, Inner classes, Multithreading, I/O Stream, Networking, AWT, Swing, Reflection, Collection, etc.

2) Java EE (Java Enterprise Edition)

It is an enterprise platform which is mainly used to develop web and enterprise applications. It is built on the top of the Java SE platform. It includes topics like Servlet, JSP, Web Services, EJB, JPA, etc.

3) Java ME (Java Micro Edition)

It is a micro platform which is mainly used to develop mobile applications.

4) JavaFX

It is used to develop rich internet applications. It uses a light-weight user interface API.

History of Java

1. History of Java
2. Java Version History

The history of Java is very interesting. Java was originally designed for interactive television, but it was too advanced technology for the digital cable television industry at the time. The history of java starts with Green Team. Java team members (also known as **Green Team**), initiated this project to develop a language for digital devices such as set-top boxes, televisions, etc. However, it was suited for internet programming. Later, Java technology was incorporated by Netscape.

The principles for creating Java programming were "Simple, Robust, Portable, Platform-independent, Secured, High Performance, Multithreaded, Architecture Neutral, Object-Oriented, Interpreted and Dynamic".

Currently, Java is used in internet programming, mobile devices, games, e-business solutions, etc. There are given the significant points that describe the history of Java.

1) **James Gosling**, **Mike Sheridan**, and **Patrick Naughton** initiated the Java language project in June 1991. The small team of sun engineers called **Green Team**.

2) Originally designed for small, embedded systems in electronic appliances like set-top boxes.

3) Firstly, it was called **"Greentalk"** by James Gosling, and file extension was .gt.

4) After that, it was called **Oak** and was developed as a part of the Green project.

Why Java named "Oak"?

5) **Why Oak?** Oak is a symbol of strength and chosen as a national tree of many countries like U.S.A., France, Germany, Romania, etc.

6) In 1995, Oak was renamed as **"Java"** because it was already a trademark by Oak Technologies.

Why Java Programming named "Java"?

7) **Why had they chosen java name for java language?** The team gathered to choose a new name. The suggested words were "dynamic", "revolutionary", "Silk", "jolt", "DNA", etc. They wanted something that reflected the essence of the technology: revolutionary, dynamic, lively, cool, unique, and easy to spell and fun to say.

According to James Gosling, "Java was one of the top choices along with **Silk**". Since Java was so unique, most of the team members preferred Java than other names.

8) Java is an island of Indonesia where first coffee was produced (called java coffee).

9) Notice that Java is just a name, not an acronym.

10) Initially developed by James Gosling at Sun Microsystems (which is now a subsidiary of Oracle Corporation) and released in 1995.

11) In 1995, Time magazine called **Java one of the Ten Best Products of 1995**.

12) JDK 1.0 released in(January 23, 1996).

Java Version History

Many java versions have been released till now. The current stable release of Java is Java SE 10.

1. JDK Alpha and Beta (1995)
2. JDK 1.0 (23rd Jan 1996)
3. JDK 1.1 (19th Feb 1997)
4. J2SE 1.2 (8th Dec 1998)
5. J2SE 1.3 (8th May 2000)
6. J2SE 1.4 (6th Feb 2002)
7. J2SE 5.0 (30th Sep 2004)
8. Java SE 6 (11th Dec 2006)
9. Java SE 7 (28th July 2011)
10. Java SE 8 (18th March 2014)
11. Java SE 9 (21st Sep 2017)
12. Java SE 10 (20th March 2018)

Difference between JDK, JRE, and JVM

1. A summary of JVM
2. Java Runtime Environment (JRE)
3. Java Development Kit (JDK)

We must understand the differences between JDK, JRE, and JVM before proceeding further to Java. See the brief overview of JVM here.

If you want to get the detailed knowledge of Java Virtual Machine, move to the next page. Firstly, let's see the differences between the JDK, JRE, and JVM.

JVM

JVM (Java Virtual Machine) is an abstract machine. It is called a virtual machine because it doesn't physically exist. It is a specification that provides a runtime environment in which Java bytecode can be executed. It can also run those programs which are written in other languages and compiled to Java bytecode.

JVMs are available for many hardware and software platforms. JVM, JRE, and JDK are platform dependent because the configuration of each OS is different from each other. However, Java is platform independent. There are three notions of the JVM: *specification*, *implementation*, and *instance*.

The JVM performs the following main tasks:

- Loads code
- Verifies code
- Executes code
- Provides runtime environment

More Details.

JRE

JRE is an acronym for Java Runtime Environment. It is also written as Java RTE. The Java Runtime Environment is a set of software tools which are used for developing Java applications. It is used to provide the runtime environment. It is the implementation of JVM. It physically exists. It contains a set of libraries + other files that JVM uses at runtime.

The implementation of JVM is also actively released by other companies besides Sun Micro Systems.

JDK

JDK is an acronym for Java Development Kit. The Java Development Kit (JDK) is a software development environment which is used to develop Java applications and applets. It physically exists. It contains JRE + development tools.

JDK is an implementation of any one of the below given Java Platforms released by Oracle Corporation:

- Standard Edition Java Platform
- Enterprise Edition Java Platform
- Micro Edition Java Platform

The JDK contains a private Java Virtual Machine (JVM) and a few other resources such as an interpreter/loader (java), a compiler (javac), an archiver (jar), a documentation generator (Javadoc), etc. to complete the development of a Java Application.

More Details.

Oracle Corporation is going to release Java SE 9 around the end of March 2017. In this post, I'm going to discuss "Java 9 Features" briefly with some examples.

1. Java 9 REPL (JShell)

Oracle Corp has introduced a new tool called "jshell". It stands for Java Shell and also known as REPL (Read Evaluate Print Loop). It is used to execute and test any Java Constructs like class, interface, enum, object, statements etc. very easily.

We can download JDK 9 EA (Early Access) software from
https://jdk9.java.net/download/

```
|  For an introduction type: /help intro


jshell> int a = 10
a ==> 10

jshell> System.out.println("a value = " + a )
a value = 10
```
If you want to know more about REPL tool, Please go through Java 9 REPL Basics (Part-1) and Java 9 REPL Features (Part-2).

2. Factory Methods for Immutable List, Set, Map and Map.Entry

Oracle Corp has introduced some convenient factory methods to create Immutable List, Set, Map and Map.Entry objects. These utility methods are used to create empty or non-empty Collection objects.

In Java SE 8 and earlier versions, We can use Collections class utility methods like `unmodifiableXXX` to create Immutable Collection objects. For instance, if we want to create an Immutable List, then we can use Collections.unmodifiableList met,hod.

However these `Collections.unmodifiableXXX` methods are very tedious and verbose approach. To overcome those shortcomings, Oracle corp has added couple of utility methods to List, Set and Map interfaces.

List and Set interfaces have "of()" methods to create an empty or no-empty Immutable List or Set objects as shown below:

Empty List Example

```
List immutableList = List.of();
```
Non-Empty List Example

```
List immutableList = List.of("one","two","three");
```
Map has two set of methods: of() methods and ofEntries() methods to create an Immutable Map object and an Immutable Map.Entry object respectively.

Empty Map Example

```
jshell> Map emptyImmutableMap = Map.of()
emptyImmutableMap ==> {}
```
Non-Empty Map Example

```
jshell> Map nonemptyImmutableMap = Map.of(1, "one", 2, "two", 3, "three")
nonemptyImmutableMap ==> {2=two, 3=three, 1=one}
```
If you want to read more about these utility methods, please go through the following links:

- Java 9 Factory Methods for Immutable List
- Java 9 Factory Methods for Immutable Set
- Java 9 Factory Methods for Immutable Map and Map.Entry

Private methods in Interfaces

In Java 8, we can provide method implementation in Interfaces using Default and Static methods. However we cannot create private methods in Interfaces.

To avoid redundant code and more re-usability, Oracle Corp is going to introduce private methods in Java SE 9 Interfaces. From Java SE 9 on-wards, we can write private and private static methods too in an interface using 'private' keyword.

These private methods are like other class private methods only, there is no difference between them.

```
public interface Card{

  private Long createCardID(){
    // Method implementation goes here.
```

```
    }

    private static void displayCardDetails(){
      // Method implementation goes here.
    }

}
```
If you want to read more about this new feature, please go through this link: Java 9 Private methods in Interface.

Java 9 Module System

One of the big changes or java 9 feature is the Module System. Oracle Corp is going to introduce the following features as part of **Jigsaw Project**.

- Modular JDK
- Modular Java Source Code
- Modular Run-time Images
- Encapsulate Java Internal APIs
- Java Platform Module System

Before Java SE 9 versions, we are using Monolithic Jars to develop Java-Based applications. This architecture has lot of limitations and drawbacks. To avoid all these shortcomings, Java SE 9 is coming with Module System.

JDK 9 is coming with 92 modules (may change in final release). We can use JDK Modules and also we can create our own modules as shown below:

Simple Module Example

```
module com.foo.bar { }
```
Here We are using 'module' to create a simple module. Each module has a name, related code and other resources.

To read more details about this new architecture and hands-on experience, please go through my original tutorials here:

- Java 9 Module System Basics
- Java 9 Module Examples using command prompt
- Java 9 Hello World Module Example using Eclipse IDE

Process API Improvements

Java SE 9 is coming with some improvements in Process API. They have added couple new classes and methods to ease the controlling and managing of OS processes.

Two new interfcase in Process API:

- java.lang.ProcessHandle
- java.lang.ProcessHandle.Info

Process API example

```
ProcessHandle currentProcess = ProcessHandle.current();
System.out.println("Current Process Id: = " +
currentProcess.getPid());
```

If you want to read more about this new API, please go through my original tutorial at: Java SE 9: Process API Improvements.

Try With Resources Improvement

We know, Java SE 7 has introduced a new exception handling construct: Try-With-Resources to manage resources automatically. The main goal of this new statement is "Automatic Better Resource Management".

Java SE 9 is going to provide some improvements to this statement to avoid some more verbosity and improve some Readability.

Java SE 7 example

```
void testARM_Before_Java9() throws IOException{
 BufferedReader reader1 = new BufferedReader(new FileReader("journaldev.txt"));
 try (BufferedReader reader2 = reader1) {
   System.out.println(reader2.readLine());
 }
}
```

Java 9 example

```
void testARM_Java9() throws IOException{
 BufferedReader reader1 = new BufferedReader(new FileReader("journaldev.txt"));
 try (reader1) {
   System.out.println(reader1.readLine());
 }
}
```

To read more about this new feature, please go through my original tutorial at: Java 9 Try-With-Resources Improvements

CompletableFuture API Improvements

In Java SE 9, Oracle Corp is going to improve CompletableFuture API to solve some problems raised in Java SE 8. They are going add to support some delays and timeouts, some utility methods and better sub-classing.

```
Executor exe = CompletableFuture.delayedExecutor(50L,
TimeUnit.SECONDS);
```
Here delayedExecutor() is static utility method used to return a new Executor that submits a task to the default executor after the given delay.

To read more about this feature, please go through my original tutorial at: Java SE 9: CompletableFuture API Improvements

Reactive Streams

Now-a-days, Reactive Programming has become very popular in developing applications to get some beautiful benefits. Scala, Play, Akka etc. Frameworks has already integrated Reactive Streams and getting many benefits. Oracle Corps is also introducing new Reactive Streams API in Java SE 9.

Java SE 9 Reactive Streams API is a Publish/Subscribe Framework to implement Asynchronous, Scalable and Parallel applications very easily using Java language.

Java SE 9 has introduced the following API to develop Reactive Streams in Java-based applications.

- java.util.concurrent.Flow
- java.util.concurrent.Flow.Publisher
- java.util.concurrent.Flow.Subscriber
- java.util.concurrent.Flow.Processor

Read more at Java 9 Reactive Streams.

Diamond Operator for Anonymous Inner Class

We know, Java SE 7 has introduced one new feature: Diamond Operator to avoid redundant code and verbosity, to improve readability. However in Java SE 8, Oracle Corp (Java Library Developer) has found that some limitation in the use of Diamond operator with Anonymous Inner Class. They have fixed that issues and going to release as part of Java 9.

```
public List getEmployee(String empid){
```

```
    // Code to get Employee details from Data Store
    return new List(emp){ };
}
```

Here we are using just "List" without specifying the type parameter. To read more details about this improvement, please go through my original tutorial at: **Java SE 9: Diamond Operator improvements for Anonymous Inner Class**

Optional Class Improvements

In Java SE 9, Oracle Corp has added some useful new methods to java.util.Optional class. Here I'm going to discuss about one of those methods with some simple example: stream method

If a value present in the given Optional object, this stream() method returns a sequential Stream with that value. Otherwise, it returns an Empty Stream.

They have added "stream()" method to work on Optional objects lazily as shown below:

```
Stream<Optional> emp = getEmployee(id)
Stream empStream = emp.flatMap(Optional::stream)
```

Here Optional.stream() method is used convert a Stream of Optional of Employee object into a Stream of Employee so that we can work on this result lazily in the result code.

To understand more about this feature with more examples and to read more new methods added to Optional class, please go through my original tutorial at: **Java SE 9: Optional Class Improvements**

Stream API Improvements

In Java SE 9, Oracle Corp has added four useful new methods to java.util.Stream interface. As Stream is an interface, all those new implemented methods are default methods. Two of them are very important: dropWhile and takeWhile methods

If you are familiar with Scala Language or any Functions programming language, you will definitely know about these methods. These are very useful methods in writing some functional style code. Let us discuss about takeWhile utility method here.

This takeWhile() takes a predicate as an argument and returns a Stream of subset of the given Stream values until that Predicate returns false for the first time. If first value does NOT satisfy that Predicate, it just returns an empty Stream.

```
jshell> Stream.of(1,2,3,4,5,6,7,8,9,10).takeWhile(i -> i <
5 )
                    .forEach(System.out::println);
1
2
3
4
```

To read more about takeWhile and dropWhile methods and other new methods, please go through my original tutorial at: **Java SE 9: Stream API Improvements**

Enhanced @Deprecated annotation

In Java SE 8 and earlier versions, @Deprecated annotation is just a Marker interface without any methods. It is used to mark a Java API that is a class, field, method, interface, constructor, enum etc.

In Java SE 9, Oracle Corp has enhanced @Deprecated annotation to provide more information about deprecated API and also provide a **Tool** to analyse an application's static usage of deprecated APIs. They have add two methods to this Deprecated interface: **forRemoval** and **since** to serve this information.

Read my original tutorial at: **Java SE 9: Enhanced @Deprecated annotation** to see some useful examples.

HTTP 2 Client

In Java SE 9, Oracle Corp is going to release New HTTP 2 Client API to support HTTP/2 protocol and WebSocket features. As existing or Legacy HTTP Client API has numerous issues (like supports HTTP/1.1 protocol and does not support HTTP/2 protocol and WebSocket, works only in Blocking mode and lot of performance issues.), they are replacing this HttpURLConnection API with new HTTP client.

They are going to introduce new HTTP 2 Client API under "java.net.http" package. It supports both HTTP/1.1 and HTTP/2 protocols. It supports both Synchronous (Blocking Mode) and Asynchronous Modes. It supports Asynchronous Mode using WebSocket API.

We can see this new API at:
http://download.java.net/java/jdk9/docs/api/java/net/http/package-summary.html

HTTP 2 Client Example

```
jshell> import java.net.http.*

jshell> import static java.net.http.HttpRequest.*

jshell> import static java.net.http.HttpResponse.*

jshell> URI uri = new
URI("http://rams4java.blogspot.co.uk/2016/05/java-
news.html")
uri ==> http://rams4java.blogspot.co.uk/2016/05/java-
news.html

jshell> HttpResponse response =
HttpRequest.create(uri).body(noBody()).GET().response()
response ==> java.net.http.HttpResponseImpl@79efed2d

jshell> System.out.println("Response was " +
response.body(asString()))
```
Please go through my original tutorial at: **Java SE 9: HTTP 2 Client** to understand HTTP/2 protocol & WebSocket, Benefits of new API and Drawbacks of OLD API with some useful examples.

Multi-Resolution Image API

In Java SE 9, Oracle Corp is going to introduce a new Multi-Resolution Image API. Important interface in this API is MultiResolutionImage . It is available in java.awt.image package.

MultiResolutionImage encapsulates a set of images with different Height and Widths (that is different resolutions) and allows us to query them with our requirements.

Miscellaneous Java 9 Features

In this section, I will just list out some miscellaneous Java SE 9 New Features. I'm NOT saying these are less important features. They are also important and useful to understand them very well with some useful examples.

As of now, I did not get enough information about these features. That's why I am going list them here for brief understanding. I will pickup these Features one by one and add to above section with a brief discussion and example. And final write a separate tutorial later.

- GC (Garbage Collector) Improvements

- Stack-Walking API
- Filter Incoming Serialization Data
- Deprecate the Applet API
- Indify String Concatenation
- Enhanced Method Handles
- Java Platform Logging API and Service
- Compact Strings
- Parser API for Nashorn
- Javadoc Search
- HTML5 Javadoc

Java 9 Reactive Streams

Reactive Streams is about asynchronous processing of stream, so there should be a **Publisher** and a **Subscriber**. The Publisher publishes the stream of data and the Subscriber consumes the data.

Sometimes we have to transform the data between Publisher and Subscriber. **Processor** is the entity sitting between the end publisher and subscriber to transform the data received from publisher so that subscriber can understand it. We can have a chain of processors.

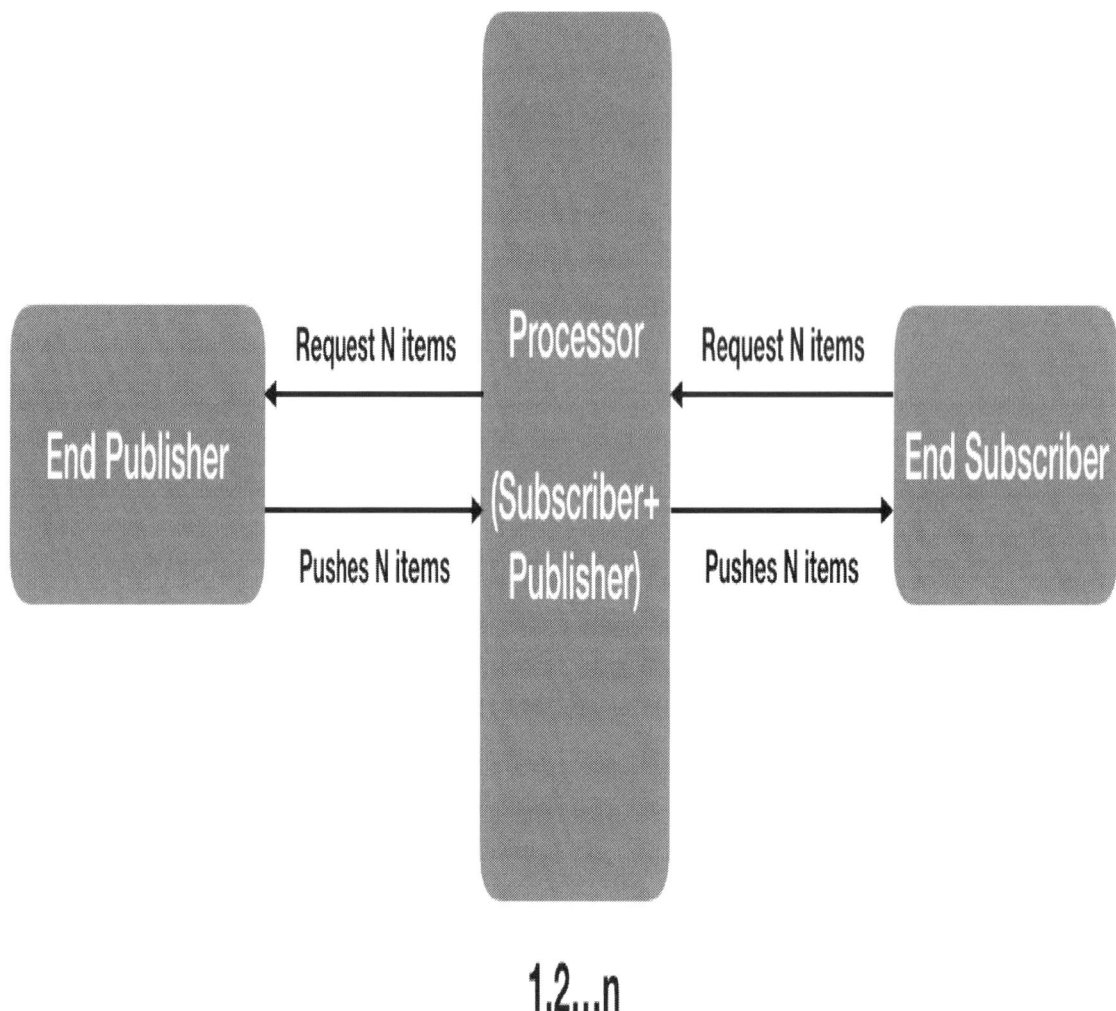

It's very clear from the above image that Processor works both as Subscriber and a Publisher.

Java 9 Flow API

Java 9 Flow API implements the **Reactive Streams Specification**. Flow API is a combination of Iterator and Observer pattern. Iterator works on pull model where application pulls items from the source, whereas Observer works on push model and reacts when item is pushed from source to application.

Java 9 Flow API subscriber can request for N items while subscribing to the publisher. Then the items are pushed from publisher to subscriber until there are no more items left to push or some error occurs.

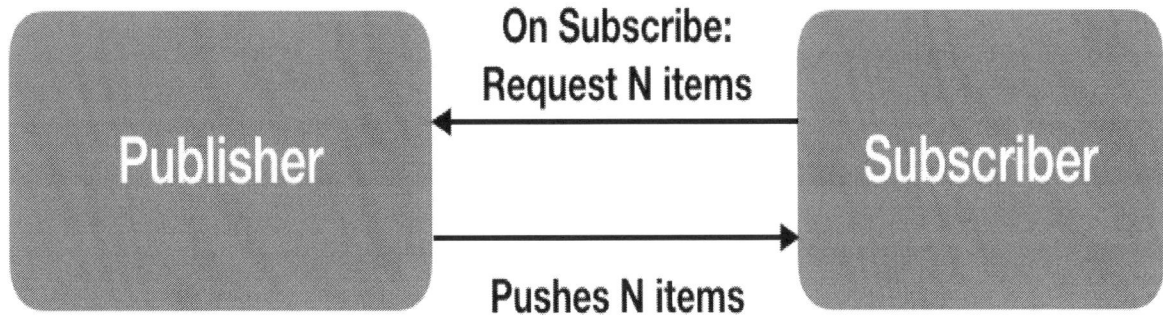

Java 9 Flow API Classes and Interfaces

Let's have a quick look at Flow API classes and interfaces.

- `java.util.concurrent.Flow`: This is the main class of Flow API. This class encapsulates all the important interfaces of the Flow API. This is a final class and we can't extend it.
- `java.util.concurrent.Flow.Publisher`: This is a functional interface and every publisher has to implement it's subscribe method to add the given subscriber to receive messages.
- `java.util.concurrent.Flow.Subscriber`: Every subscriber has to implement this interface. The methods in the subscriber are invoked in strict sequential order. There are four methods in this interface:

    - `onSubscribe`: This is the first method to get invoked when subscriber is subscribed to receive messages by publisher. Usually we invoke `subscription.request` to start receiving items from processor.
    - `onNext`: This method gets invoked when an item is received from publisher, this is where we implement our business logic to process the stream and then request for more data from publisher.
    - `onError`: This method is invoked when an irrecoverable error occurs, we can do cleanup taks in this method, such as closing database connection.
    - `onComplete`: This is like finally method and gets invoked when no other items are being produced by publisher and publisher is closed. We can use it to send notification of successful processing of stream.

    `java.util.concurrent.Flow.Subscription`: This is used to create asynchronous non-blocking link between publisher and subscriber. Subscriber invokes its `request` method to demand items from publisher. It also has `cancel` method to cancel the subscription i.e. closing the link between publisher and subscriber.

23

`java.util.concurrent.Flow.Processor`: This interface extends both Publisher and Subscriber, this is used to transform the message between publisher and subscriber.

`java.util.concurrent.SubmissionPublisher`: A Publisher implementation that asynchronously issues submitted items to current subscribers until it is closed. It uses Executor framework We will use this class in reactive stream examples to add subscriber and then submit items to them.

Java 9 Reactive Stream Example

Let's start with a simple example where we will implement Flow API Subscriber interface and use SubmissionPublisher to create publisher and send messages.

Stream Data

Let's say we have an Employee class that will be used to create the stream message to be sent from publisher to subscriber.

```
package com.journaldev.reactive.beans;

public class Employee {

    private int id;
    private String name;

    public int getId() {
        return id;
    }
    public void setId(int id) {
        this.id = id;
    }
    public String getName() {
        return name;
    }
    public void setName(String name) {
        this.name = name;
    }

    public Employee(int i, String s) {
        this.id = i;
        this.name = s;
    }

    public Employee() {
    }

    @Override
    public String toString() {
```

```
                return "[id="+id+",name="+name+"]";
        }
}
```
We also have a utility class to create a list of employees for our example.

```
package com.journaldev.reactive_streams;

import java.util.ArrayList;
import java.util.List;

import com.journaldev.reactive.beans.Employee;

public class EmpHelper {

        public static List<Employee> getEmps() {

                Employee e1 = new Employee(1, "Pankaj");
                Employee e2 = new Employee(2, "David");
                Employee e3 = new Employee(3, "Lisa");
                Employee e4 = new Employee(4, "Ram");
                Employee e5 = new Employee(5, "Anupam");

                List<Employee> emps = new ArrayList<>();
                emps.add(e1);
                emps.add(e2);
                emps.add(e3);
                emps.add(e4);
                emps.add(e5);

                return emps;
        }

}
```

Subscriber

```
package com.journaldev.reactive_streams;

import java.util.concurrent.Flow.Subscriber;
import java.util.concurrent.Flow.Subscription;

import com.journaldev.reactive.beans.Employee;

public class MySubscriber implements Subscriber<Employee> {

        private Subscription subscription;

        private int counter = 0;
```

```java
        @Override
        public void onSubscribe(Subscription subscription) {
            System.out.println("Subscribed");
            this.subscription = subscription;
            this.subscription.request(1); //requesting data from publisher
            System.out.println("onSubscribe requested 1 item");
        }

        @Override
        public void onNext(Employee item) {
            System.out.println("Processing Employee "+item);
            counter++;
            this.subscription.request(1);
        }

        @Override
        public void onError(Throwable e) {
            System.out.println("Some error happened");
            e.printStackTrace();
        }

        @Override
        public void onComplete() {
            System.out.println("All Processing Done");
        }

        public int getCounter() {
            return counter;
        }

}
```

- `Subscription` variable to keep reference so that request can be made in `onNext` method.
- `counter` variable to keep count of number of items processed, notice that it's value is increased in onNext method. This will be used in our main method to wait for execution to finish before ending the main thread.
- Subscription request is invoked in `onSubscribe` method to start the processing. Also notice that it's again called in `onNext` method after processing the item, demanding next item to process from the publisher.
- `onError` and `onComplete` doesn't have much here, but in real world scenario they should be used to perform corrective measures when error occurs or cleanup of resources when processing completes successfully.

Reactive Stream Test Program

We will use `SubmissionPublisher` as Publisher for our examples, so let's look at the test program for our reactive stream implementation.

```java
package com.journaldev.reactive_streams;

import java.util.List;
import java.util.concurrent.SubmissionPublisher;

import com.journaldev.reactive.beans.Employee;

public class MyReactiveApp {

    public static void main(String args[]) throws InterruptedException {

        // Create Publisher
        SubmissionPublisher<Employee> publisher = new SubmissionPublisher<>();

        // Register Subscriber
        MySubscriber subs = new MySubscriber();
        publisher.subscribe(subs);

        List<Employee> emps = EmpHelper.getEmps();

        // Publish items
        System.out.println("Publishing Items to Subscriber");
        emps.stream().forEach(i -> publisher.submit(i));

        // logic to wait till processing of all messages are over
        while (emps.size() != subs.getCounter()) {
            Thread.sleep(10);
        }
        // close the Publisher
        publisher.close();

        System.out.println("Exiting the app");

    }

}
```

The most important piece of above code is `subscribe` and `submit` methods invocation of publisher. We should always close publisher to avoid any memory leaks.

We will get following output when above program is executed.

```
Subscribed
Publishing Items to Subscriber
onSubscribe requested 1 item
```

```
Processing Employee [id=1,name=Pankaj]
Processing Employee [id=2,name=David]
Processing Employee [id=3,name=Lisa]
Processing Employee [id=4,name=Ram]
Processing Employee [id=5,name=Anupam]
Exiting the app
All Processing Done
```
Note that if we won't have logic for main method to wait before all the items are processed, then we will get unwanted results.

Message Transformation Example

Processor is used to transform the message between a publisher and subscriber. Let's say we have another subscriber which is expecting a different type of message to process. Let's say this new message type is `Freelancer`.

```
package com.journaldev.reactive.beans;

public class Freelancer extends Employee {

    private int fid;

    public int getFid() {
        return fid;
    }

    public void setFid(int fid) {
        this.fid = fid;
    }

    public Freelancer(int id, int fid, String name) {
        super(id, name);
        this.fid = fid;
    }

    @Override
    public String toString() {
        return
"[id="+super.getId()+",name="+super.getName()+",fid="+fid+"]";
    }
}
```
We have a new subscriber to consume Freelancer stream data.

```
package com.journaldev.reactive_streams;

import java.util.concurrent.Flow.Subscriber;
import java.util.concurrent.Flow.Subscription;
```

```java
import com.journaldev.reactive.beans.Freelancer;

public class MyFreelancerSubscriber implements Subscriber<Freelancer> {

    private Subscription subscription;

    private int counter = 0;

    @Override
    public void onSubscribe(Subscription subscription) {
        System.out.println("Subscribed for Freelancer");
        this.subscription = subscription;
        this.subscription.request(1); //requesting data from publisher
        System.out.println("onSubscribe requested 1 item for Freelancer");
    }

    @Override
    public void onNext(Freelancer item) {
        System.out.println("Processing Freelancer "+item);
        counter++;
        this.subscription.request(1);
    }

    @Override
    public void onError(Throwable e) {
        System.out.println("Some error happened in MyFreelancerSubscriber");
        e.printStackTrace();
    }

    @Override
    public void onComplete() {
        System.out.println("All Processing Done for MyFreelancerSubscriber");
    }

    public int getCounter() {
        return counter;
    }

}
```

Processor

The important part is the implementation of `Processor` interface. Since we want to utilize the `SubmissionPublisher`, we would extend it and use it wherever applicable.

```java
package com.journaldev.reactive_streams;

import java.util.concurrent.Flow.Processor;
import java.util.concurrent.Flow.Subscription;
import java.util.concurrent.SubmissionPublisher;
import java.util.function.Function;

import com.journaldev.reactive.beans.Employee;
import com.journaldev.reactive.beans.Freelancer;

public class MyProcessor extends
SubmissionPublisher<Freelancer> implements Processor<Employee,
Freelancer> {

    private Subscription subscription;
    private Function<Employee,Freelancer> function;

    public MyProcessor(Function<Employee,Freelancer> function) {
        super();
        this.function = function;
    }

    @Override
    public void onSubscribe(Subscription subscription) {
        this.subscription = subscription;
        subscription.request(1);
    }

    @Override
    public void onNext(Employee emp) {
        submit((Freelancer) function.apply(emp));
        subscription.request(1);
    }

    @Override
    public void onError(Throwable e) {
        e.printStackTrace();
    }

    @Override
    public void onComplete() {
        System.out.println("Done");
    }

}
```

- `Function` will be used to convert Employee object to Freelancer object.

- We will convert incoming Employee message to Freelancer message in `onNext` method and then use SubmissionPublisher submit method to send it to the subscriber.
- Since Processor works as both subscriber and publisher, we can create a chain of processors between end publishers and subscribers.

Message Transformation Test

```
package com.journaldev.reactive_streams;

import java.util.List;
import java.util.concurrent.SubmissionPublisher;

import com.journaldev.reactive.beans.Employee;
import com.journaldev.reactive.beans.Freelancer;

public class MyReactiveAppWithProcessor {

    public static void main(String[] args) throws InterruptedException {
        // Create End Publisher
        SubmissionPublisher<Employee> publisher = new SubmissionPublisher<>();

        // Create Processor
        MyProcessor transformProcessor = new MyProcessor(s -> {
            return new Freelancer(s.getId(), s.getId() + 100, s.getName());
        });

        //Create End Subscriber
        MyFreelancerSubscriber subs = new MyFreelancerSubscriber();

        //Create chain of publisher, processor and subscriber
        publisher.subscribe(transformProcessor); // publisher to processor
        transformProcessor.subscribe(subs); // processor to subscriber

        List<Employee> emps = EmpHelper.getEmps();

        // Publish items
        System.out.println("Publishing Items to Subscriber");
        emps.stream().forEach(i -> publisher.submit(i));
```

```
                // Logic to wait for messages processing to finish
                while (emps.size() != subs.getCounter()) {
                    Thread.sleep(10);
                }

                // Closing publishers
                publisher.close();
                transformProcessor.close();

                System.out.println("Exiting the app");
        }

}
```

Read the comments in the program to properly understand it, most important change is the creation of producer-processor-subscriber chain. We will get following output when above program is executed.

```
Subscribed for Freelancer
Publishing Items to Subscriber
onSubscribe requested 1 item for Freelancer
Processing Freelancer [id=1,name=Pankaj,fid=101]
Processing Freelancer [id=2,name=David,fid=102]
Processing Freelancer [id=3,name=Lisa,fid=103]
Processing Freelancer [id=4,name=Ram,fid=104]
Processing Freelancer [id=5,name=Anupam,fid=105]
Exiting the app
All Processing Done for MyFreelancerSubscriber
Done
```

Cancel Subscription

We can use Subscription cancel method to stop receiving message in subscriber. Note that if we cancel the subscription, then subscriber will not receive onComplete or onError signal.

Here is a sample code where subscriber is consuming only 3 messages and then canceling the subscription.

```
@Override
public void onNext(Employee item) {
    System.out.println("Processing Employee "+item);
    counter++;
    if(counter==3) {
        this.subscription.cancel();
        return;
    }
    this.subscription.request(1);
}
```

Note that in this case, our logic to halt main thread before all the messages are processed will go into infinite loop. We can add some additional logic for this scenario, may be some global variable to look for if subscriber has stopped processing or canceled subscription.

Back Pressure

When publisher is producing messages in much faster rate than it's being consumed by subscriber, back pressure gets built. Flow API doesn't provide any mechanism to signal about back pressure or to deal with it. But we can devise our own strategy to deal with it, such as fine tuning the subscriber or reducing the message producing rate.

Introduction

In RxJava it is not difficult to get into a situation in which an Observable is emitting items more rapidly than an operator or subscriber can consume them. This presents the problem of what to do with such a growing backlog of unconsumed items.

For example, imagine using the `zip` operator to zip together two infinite Observables, one of which emits items twice as frequently as the other. A naive implementation of the `zip` operator would have to maintain an ever-expanding buffer of items emitted by the faster Observable to eventually combine with items emitted by the slower one. This could cause RxJava to seize an unwieldy amount of system resources.
There are a variety of strategies with which you can exercise flow control and backpressure in RxJava in order to alleviate the problems caused when a quickly-producing Observable meets a slow-consuming observer. This page explains some of these strategies, and also shows you how you can design your own Observables and Observable operators to respect requests for flow control.

Hot and cold Observables, and multicasted Observables

A *cold* Observable emits a particular sequence of items, but can begin emitting this sequence when its Observer finds it to be convenient, and at whatever rate the Observer desires, without disrupting the integrity of the sequence. For example if you convert a static Iterable into an Observable, that Observable will emit the same sequence of items no matter when it is later subscribed to or how frequently those items are observed. Examples of items emitted by a cold Observable might include the results of a database query, file retrieval, or web request.

A *hot* Observable begins generating items to emit immediately when it is created. Subscribers typically begin observing the sequence of items emitted by a hot Observable from somewhere in the middle of the sequence, beginning with the first item emitted by the Observable subsequent to the establishment of the subscription. Such an Observable emits items at its own pace, and it is up to its observers to keep up. Examples of items emitted by a hot Observable might include mouse & keyboard events, system events, or stock prices.

When a cold Observable is *multicast* (when it is converted into a `ConnectableObservable` and its `connect()` method is called), it effectively becomes *hot* and for the purposes of backpressure and flow-control it should be treated as a hot Observable.
Cold Observables are ideal for the reactive pull model of backpressure described below. Hot Observables typically do not cope well with a reactive pull model, and are better candidates for some of the other flow control strategies discussed on this page, such as the use of the `onBackpressureBuffer` or `onBackpressureDrop` operators, throttling, buffers, or windows.

Useful operators that avoid the need for backpressure

Your first line of defense against the problems of over-producing Observables is to use some of the ordinary set of Observable operators to reduce the number of emitted items to a more manageable number. The examples in this section will show how you might use such operators to handle a bursty Observable like the one illustrated in the following marble diagram:

By fine-tuning the parameters to these operators you can ensure that a slow-consuming observer is not overwhelmed by a fast-producing Observable.

Throttling

Operators like `sample()` or `throttleLast()`, `throttleFirst()`, and `throttleWithTimeout()` or `debounce()` allow you to regulate the rate at which an Observable emits items.
The following diagrams show how you could use each of these operators on the bursty Observable shown above.

sample (or throttleLast)

The `sample` operator periodically "dips" into the sequence and emits only the most recently emitted item during each dip:

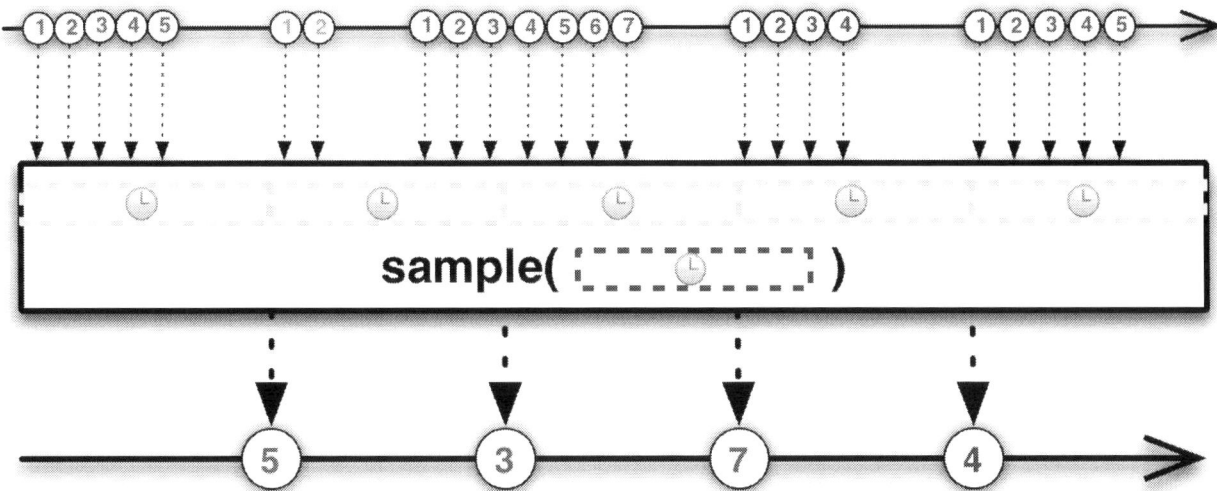

```
Observable<Integer> burstySampled = bursty.sample(500, TimeUnit.MILLISECONDS);
```

throttleFirst

The `throttleFirst` operator is similar, but emits not the most recently emitted item, but the first item that was emitted after the previous "dip":

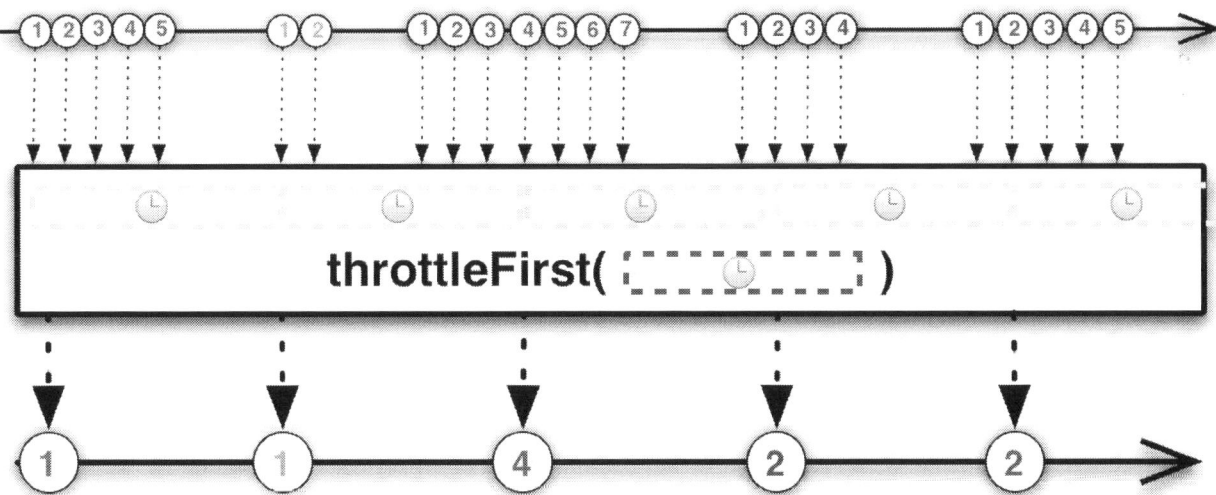

```
Observable<Integer> burstyThrottled = bursty.throttleFirst(500,
TimeUnit.MILLISECONDS);
```

debounce (or throttleWithTimeout)

The `debounce` operator emits only those items from the source Observable that are not followed by another item within a specified duration:

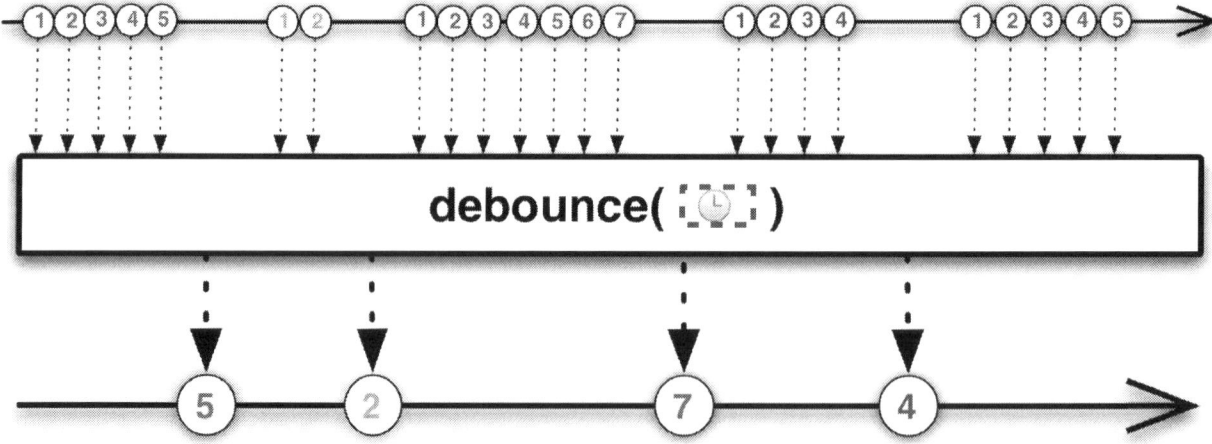

```
Observable<Integer> burstyDebounced = bursty.debounce(10, TimeUnit.MILLISECONDS);
```

Buffers and windows

You can also use an operator like `buffer()` or `window()` to collect items from the over-producing Observable and then emit them, less-frequently, as collections (or Observables) of items. The slow consumer can then decide whether to process only one particular item from each collection, to process some combination of those items, or to schedule work to be done on each item in the collection, as appropriate. The following diagrams show how you could use each of these operators on the bursty Observable shown above.

buffer

You could, for example, close and emit a buffer of items from the bursty Observable periodically, at a regular interval of time:

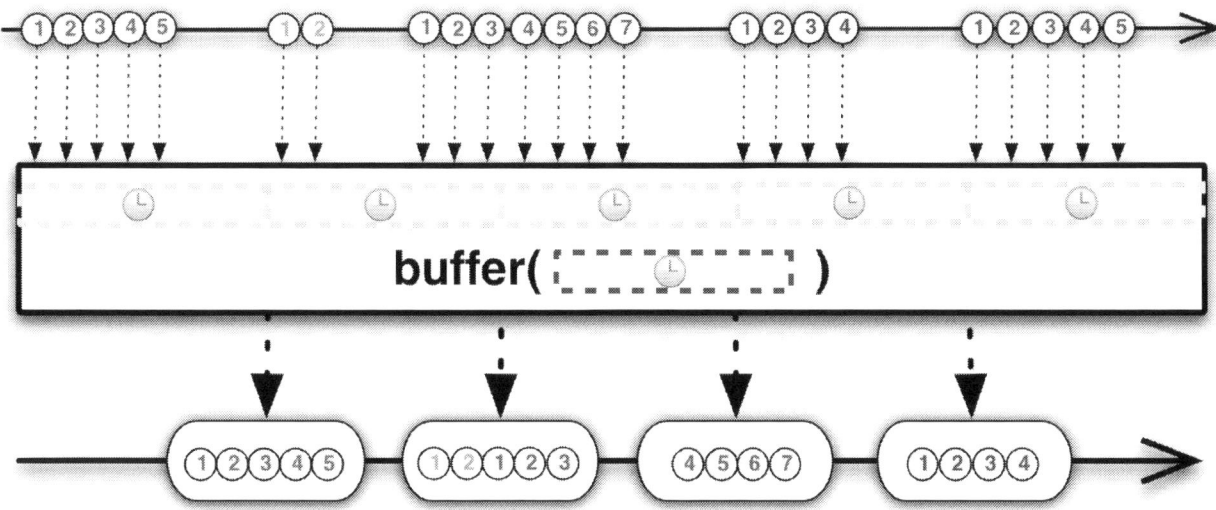

```
Observable<List<Integer>> burstyBuffered = bursty.buffer(500,
TimeUnit.MILLISECONDS);
```

Or you could get fancy, and collect items in buffers during the bursty periods and emit them at the end of each burst, by using the debounce operator to emit a buffer closing indicator to the buffer operator:

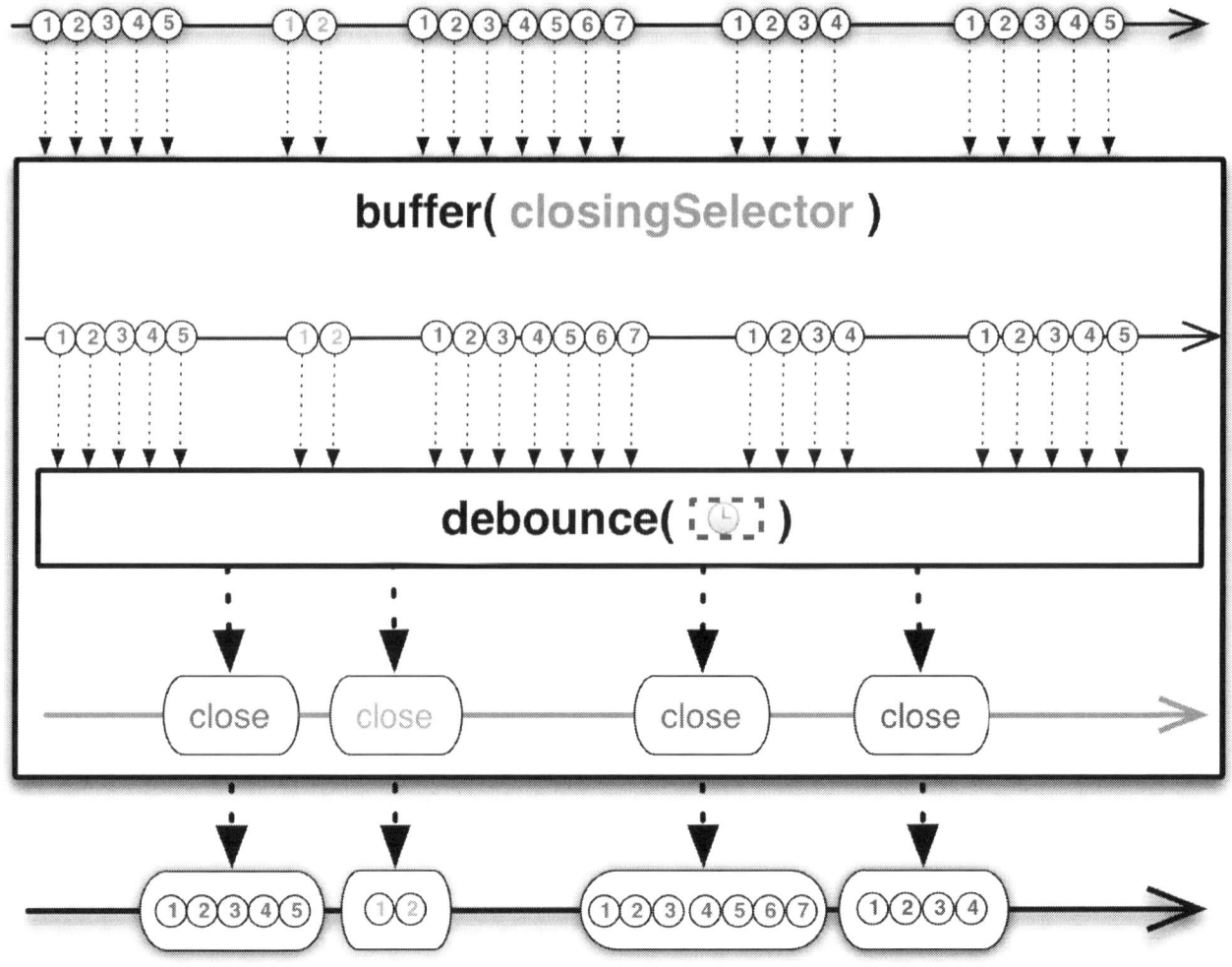

```
// we have to multicast the original bursty Observable so we can use it
// both as our source and as the source for our buffer closing selector:
Observable<Integer> burstyMulticast = bursty.publish().refCount();
// burstyDebounced will be our buffer closing selector:
Observable<Integer> burstyDebounced = burstMulticast.debounce(10,
TimeUnit.MILLISECONDS);
// and this, finally, is the Observable of buffers we're interested in:
Observable<List<Integer>> burstyBuffered =
burstyMulticast.buffer(burstyDebounced);
```

window

window is similar to buffer. One variant of window allows you to periodically emit Observable windows of items at a regular interval of time:

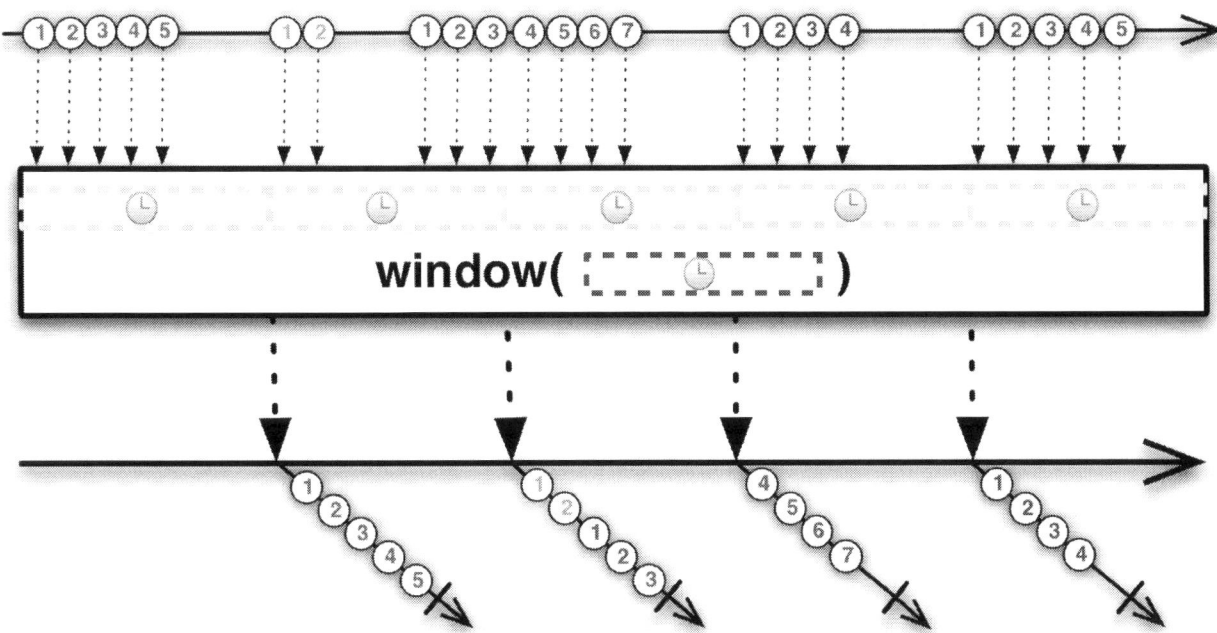

```
Observable<Observable<Integer>> burstyWindowed = bursty.window(500,
TimeUnit.MILLISECONDS);
```

You could also choose to emit a new window each time you have collected a particular number of items from the source Observable:

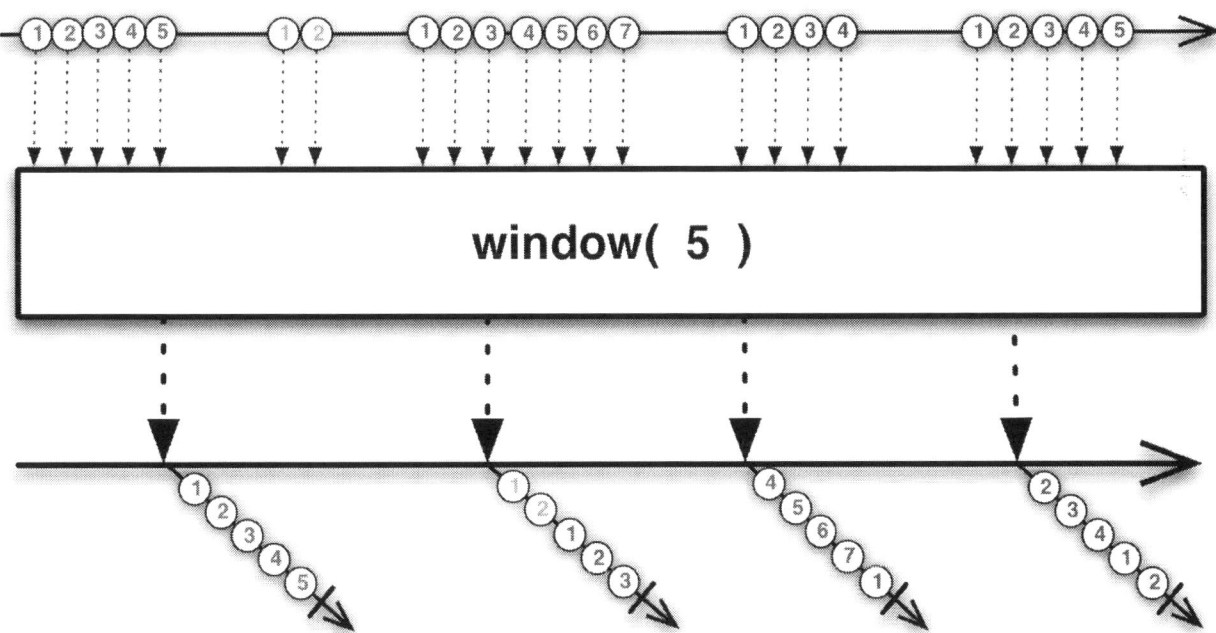

```
Observable<Observable<Integer>> burstyWindowed = bursty.window(5);
```

Callstack blocking as a flow-control alternative to backpressure

Another way of handling an overproductive Observable is to block the callstack (parking the thread that governs the overproductive Observable). This has the disadvantage of going against the "reactive" and non-blocking model of Rx. However this can be a viable option if the problematic Observable is on a thread that can be blocked safely. Currently RxJava does not expose any operators to facilitate this.

If the Observable, all of the operators that operate on it, and the observer that is subscribed to it, are all operating in the same thread, this effectively establishes a form of backpressure by means of callstack blocking. But be aware that many Observable operators do operate in distinct threads by default (the javadocs for those operators will indicate this).

How a subscriber establishes "reactive pull" backpressure

When you subscribe to an Observable with a Subscriber, you can request reactive pull backpressure by calling Subscriber.request(n) in the Subscriber's onStart() method (where *n* is the maximum number of items you want the Observable to emit before the next request() call).
Then, after handling this item (or these items) in onNext(), you can call request() again to instruct the Observable to emit another item (or items). Here is an example of a Subscriber that requests one item at a time from someObservable:

```
someObservable.subscribe(new Subscriber<t>() {
    @Override
    public void onStart() {
      request(1);
    }

    @Override
    public void onCompleted() {
      // gracefully handle sequence-complete
    }

    @Override
    public void onError(Throwable e) {
      // gracefully handle error
    }

    @Override
    public void onNext(t n) {
      // do something with the emitted item "n"
      // request another item:
```

```
        request(1);
    }
});
```

You can pass a magic number to `request`, `request(Long.MAX_VALUE)`, to disable reactive pull backpressure and to ask the Observable to emit items at its own pace. `request(0)` is a legal call, but has no effect. Passing values less than zero to `request` will cause an exception to be thrown.

Reactive pull backpressure isn't magic

Backpressure doesn't make the problem of an overproducing Observable or an underconsuming Subscriber go away. It just moves the problem up the chain of operators to a point where it can be handled better.

Let's take a closer look at the problem of the uneven `zip`.
You have two Observables, A and B, where B is inclined to emit items more frequently than A. When you try to `zip` these two Observables together, the `zip` operator combines item n from A and item n from B, but meanwhile B has also emitted items $n+1$ to $n+m$. The `zip` operator has to hold on to these items so it can combine them with items $n+1$ to $n+m$ from A as they are emitted, but meanwhile m keeps growing and so the size of the buffer needed to hold on to these items keeps increasing.
You could attach a throttling operator to B, but this would mean ignoring some of the items B emits, which might not be appropriate. What you'd really like to do is to signal to B that it needs to slow down and then let B decide how to do this in a way that maintains the integrity of its emissions.

The reactive pull backpressure model lets you do this. It creates a sort of active pull from the Subscriber in contrast to the normal passive push Observable behavior.

The `zip` operator as implemented in RxJava uses this technique. It maintains a small buffer of items for each source Observable, and it requests no more items from each source Observable than would fill its buffer. Each time `zip` emits an item, it removes the corresponding items from its buffers and requests exactly one more item from each of its source Observables.
(Many RxJava operators exercise reactive pull backpressure. Some operators do not need to use this variety of backpressure, as they operate in the same thread as the Observable they operate on, and so they exert a form of blocking backpressure simply by not giving the Observable the opportunity to emit another item until they have finished processing the previous one. For other operators, backpressure is inappropriate as they have been explicitly designed to deal with flow control in other ways. The RxJava javadocs for those operators that are methods of the Observable class indicate which ones do not use reactive pull backpressure and why.)

For this to work, though, Observables *A* and *B* must respond correctly to the request(). If an Observable has not been written to support reactive pull backpressure (such support is not a requirement for Observables), you can apply one of the following operators to it, each of which forces a simple form of backpressure behavior:

onBackpressureBuffer

> maintains a buffer of all emissions from the source Observable and emits them to downstream Subscribers according to the requests they generate

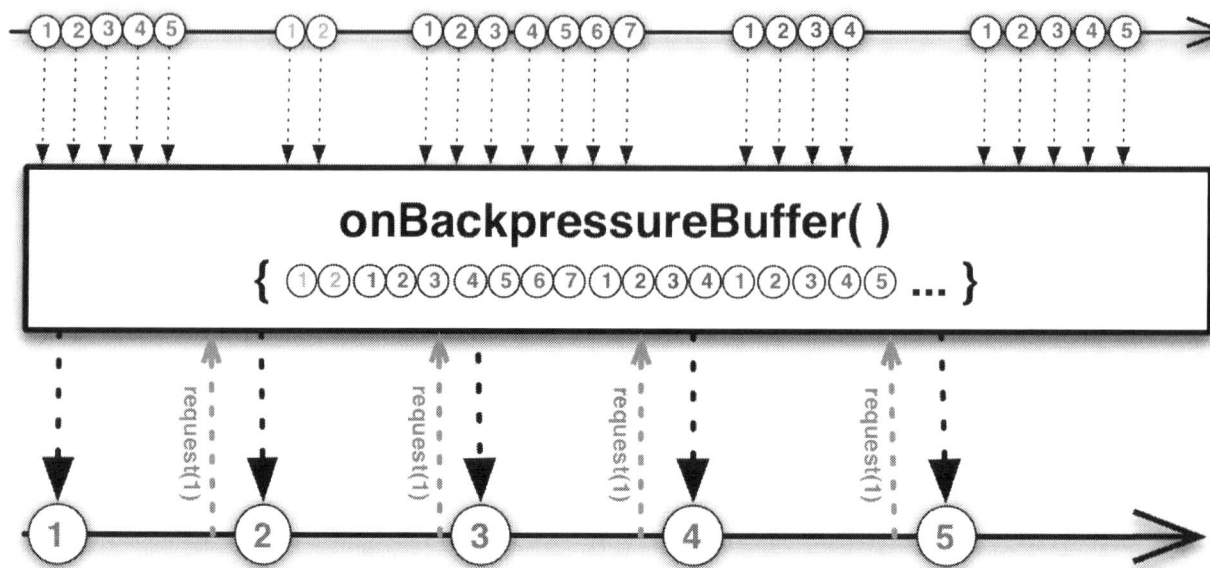

> an experimental version of this operator (not available in RxJava 1.0) allows you to set the capacity of the buffer; applying this operator will cause the resulting Observable to terminate with an error if this buffer is overrun

onBackpressureDrop

> drops emissions from the source Observable unless there is a pending request from a downstream Subscriber, in which case it will emit enough items to fulfill the request

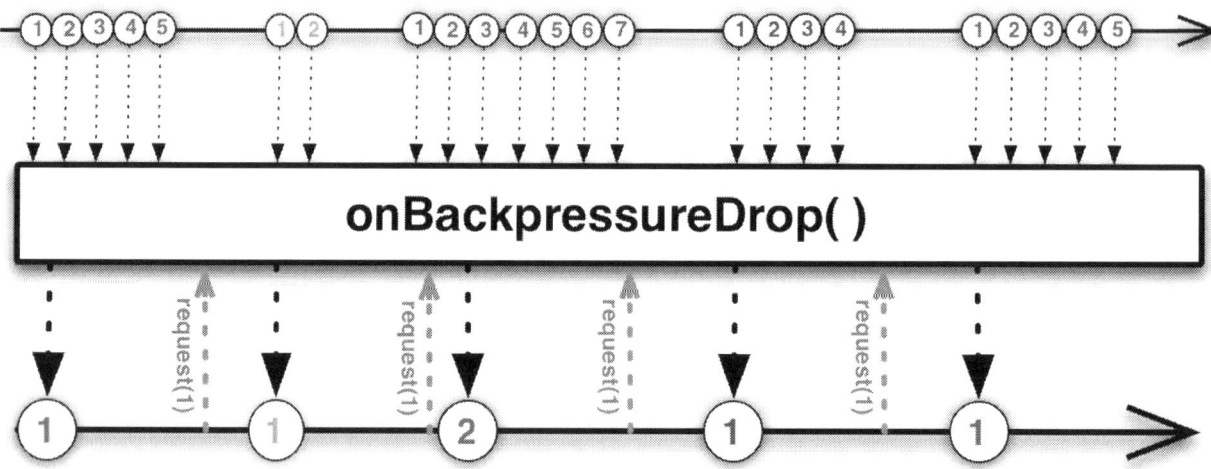

onBackpressureBlock **(experimental, not in RxJava 1.0)**

42

blocks the thread on which the source Observable is operating until such time as a Subscriber issues a `request` for items, and then unblocks the thread only so long as there are pending requests

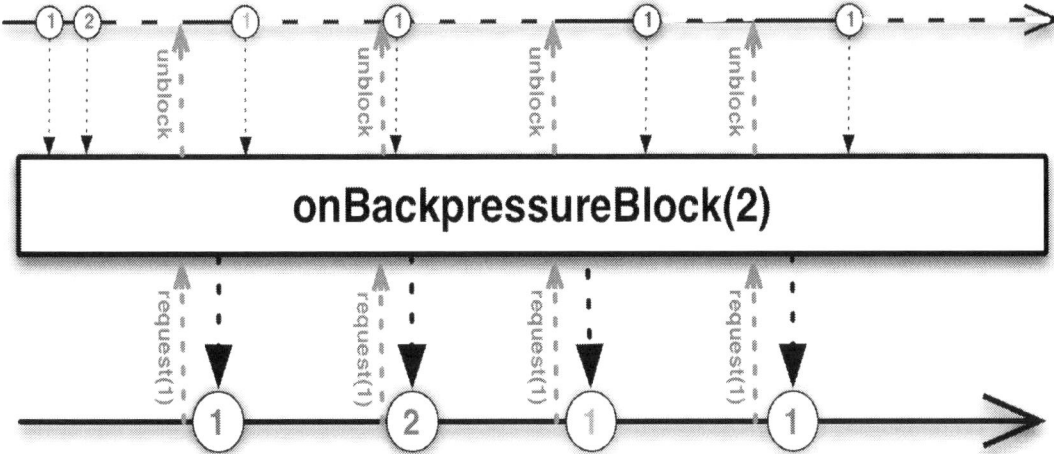

If you do not apply any of these operators to an Observable that does not support backpressure, *and* if either you as the Subscriber or some operator between you and the Observable attempts to apply reactive pull backpressure, you will encounter a `MissingBackpressureException` which you will be notified of via your `onError()` callback.

Implementing custom operators

RxJava features over 100 operators to support the most common reactive dataflow patterns. Generally, there exist a combination of operators, typically `flatMap`, `defer` and `publish`, that allow composing less common patterns with standard guarantees. When you have an uncommon pattern and you can't seem to find the right operators, try asking about it on our issue list (or Stackoverflow) first. If none of this applies to your use case, you may want to implement a custom operator. Be warned that **writing operators is hard**: when one writes an operator, the `Observable` **protocol**, **unsubscription**, **backpressure** and **concurrency** have to be taken into account and adhered to the letter.
Note that this page uses Java 8 syntax for brevity.

Considerations

Observable protocol

The `Observable` protocol states that you have to call the `Observer` methods, `onNext`, `onError` and `onCompleted` in a sequential manner. In other words, these can't be called concurrently and have to be **serialized**.

The `SerializedObserver` and `SerializedSubscriber` wrappers help you with these. Note that there are cases where this serialization has to happen.

In addition, there is an expected pattern of method calls on `Observer`:
onNext* (onError | onCompleted)?

A custom operator has to honor this pattern on its push side as well. For example, if your operator turns an `onNext` into an `onError`, the upstream has to be stopped and no further methods can be called on the downstream.

Unsubscription

The basic `Observer` method has no direct means to signal to the upstream source to stop emitting events. One either has to get the `Subscription` that the `Observable.subscribe(Observer<T>)` returns **and** be asynchronous itself.

This shortcoming was resolved by introducing the `Subscriber` class that implements the `Subscription` interface. The interface allows detecting if a `Subscriber` is no longer interested in the events.

```
interface Subscription {
    boolean isUnsubscribed();

    void unsubscribe();
}
```

In an operator, this allows active checking of the `Subscriber` state before emitting an event.

In some cases, one needs to react to the child unsubscribing immediately and not just before an emission. To support this case, the `Subscriber` class has an `add(Subscription)` method that let's the operator register `Subscriptions` of its own which get unsubscribed when the downstream calls `Subscriber.unsubscribe()`.

```
InputStream in = ...

child.add(Subscriptions.create(() -> {
    try {
        in.close();
    } catch (IOException ex) {
        RxJavaHooks.onError(ex);
    }
}));
```

Backpressure

The name of this feature is often misinterpreted. It is about telling the upstream how many `onNext` events the downstream is ready to receive. For example, if the downstream requests 5, the upstream can only call `onNext` 5 times. If the upstream can't produce 5 elements but 3, it should deliver that 3 element followed by an `onError` or `onCompleted` (depending on the operator's purpose). The requests are cumulative in the sense that if the downstream requests 5 and then 2, there is going to be 7 requests outstanding.

Backpressure handling adds a great deal of complexity to most operators: one has to track how many elements the downstream requested, how many have been delivered (by usually subtracting from the request amount) and sometimes how many elements are still available (but can't be delivered without requests). In addition, the downstream can request from any thread and is not required to happen on the common thread where otherwise the `onXXX` methods are called.

The backpressure 'channel' is established between the upstream and downstream via the `Producer` interface:

```java
interface Producer {
    void request(long n);
}
```

When an upstream supports backpressure, it will call the `Subscriber.setProducer(Producer)` method on its downstream `Subscriber` with the implementation of this interface. The downstream then can respond with `Long.MAX_VALUE` to start an unbounded streaming (effectively no backpressure between the immediate upstream and downstream) or any other positive value. A request amount of zero should be ignored.

Protocol-vise, there is no strict time when a producer can be set and it may never appear. Operators have to be ready to deal with this situation and assume the upstream runs in unbounded mode (as if `Long.MAX_VALUE` was requested).

Often, operators may implement `Producer` and `Subscription` in a single class to handle both requests and unsubscriptions from the downstream:

```java
final class MyEmitter implements Producer, Subscription {
    final Subscriber<Integer> subscriber;

    public MyEmitter(Subscriber<Integer> subscriber) {
        this.subscriber = subscriber;
    }

    @Override
    public void request(long n) {
        if (n > 0) {
            subscriber.onCompleted();
        }
    }

    @Override
    public void unsubscribe() {
        System.out.println("Unsubscribed");
    }

    @Override
    public boolean isUnsubscribed() {
        return true;
    }
}
```

```
MyEmitter emitter = new MyEmitter(child);

child.add(emitter);
child.setProducer(emitter);
```

Unfortunately, you can't implement `Producer` on a `Subscriber` because of an API oversight: `Subscriber` has a protected final `request(long n)` method to perform **deferred requesting** (store and accumulate the local request amounts until `setProducer` is called).

Concurrency

When writing operators, we mostly have to deal with concurrency via the standard Java concurrency primitives: `AtomicXXX` classes, volatile variables, `Queues`, mutual exclusion, Executors, etc.

RxJava tools

RxJava has a few support classes and utilities that let's one deal with concurrency inside operators.

The first one, `BackpressureUtils` deals with managing the cumulative requested and produced element counts for an operator. Its `getAndAddRequested()` method takes an `AtomicLong`, accumulates request amounts atomically and makes sure they don't overflow `Long.MAX_VALUE`. Its pair `produced()` subtracts the amount operators have produced, thus when both are in play, the given `AtomicLong` holds the current outstanding request amount for the downstream.
Operators sometimes have to switch between multiple sources. If a previous source didn't fulfill all its requested amount, the new source has to start with that unfulfilled amount. Otherwise as the downstream didn't receive the requested amount (and no terminal event either), it can't know when to request more. If this switch happens at an `Observable` boundary (think `concat`), the `ProducerArbiter` helps managing the change.
If there is only one item to emit eventually,
the `SingleProducer` and `SingleDelayedProducer` help work out the backpressure handling:
```
child.setProducer(new SingleProducer<>(child, 1));

// or

SingleDelayedProducer<Integer> p = new SingleDelayedProducer<>(child);

child.add(p);
child.setProducer(p);

p.setValue(2);
```

The queue-drain approach

Usually, one has to serialize calls to the onxxx methods so only one thread at a time is in any of them. The first thought, namely using synchronized blocks, is forbidden. It may cause deadlocks and unnecessary thread blocking.

Most operators, however, can use a non-blocking approach called queue-drain. It works by posting the element to be emitted (or work to be performed) onto a **queue** then atomically increments a counter. If the value before the increment was zero, it means the current thread won the right to emit the contents of the queue. Once the queue is **drained**, the counter is decremented until zero and the thread continues with other activities.

In code:

```
final AtomicInteger counter = new AtomicInteger();
final Queue<T> queue = new ConcurrentLinkedQueue<>();

public void onNext(T t) {
    queue.offer(t);
    drain();
}

void drain() {
    if (counter.getAndIncrement() == 0) {
        do {
            t = queue.poll();
            child.onNext(t);
        } while (counter.decrementAndGet() != 0);
    }
}
```

Often, the when the downstream requests some amount, that should also trigger a similar drain() call:

```
final AtomicLong requested = new AtomicLong();

@Override
public void request(long n) {
    if (n > 0) {
        BackpressureUtils.getAndAddRequested(requested, n);
        drain();
    }
}
```

Many operators do more than just draining the queue and emitting its content: they have to coordinate with the downstream to emit as many items from the queue as the downstream requested.

For example, if one writes an operator that is unbounded-in but honors the requests of the downstream, the following drain pattern will do the job:

```
// downstream's consumer
final Subscriber<? super T> child;
// temporary storage for values
```

```java
    final Queue<T> queue;
    // mutual exclusion
    final AtomicInteger counter = new AtomicInteger();
    // tracks the downstream request amount
    final AtomicLong requested = new AtomicLong();

    // no more values expected from upstream
    volatile boolean done;
    // the upstream error if any
    Throwable error;

    void drain() {
        if (counter.getAndIncrement() != 0) {
            return;
        }

        int missed = 1;
        Subscriber<? super T> child = this.child;
        Queue<T> queue = this.queue;

        for (;;) {
            long requests = requested.get();
            long emission = 0L;

            while (emission != requests) { // don't emit more than requested
                if (child.isUnsubscribed()) {
                    return;
                }

                boolean stop = done;  // order matters here!
                T t = queue.poll();
                boolean empty = t == null;

                // if no more values, emit an error or completion event
                if (stop && empty) {
                    Throwable ex = error;
                    if (ex != null) {
                        child.onError(ex);
                    } else {
                        child.onCompleted();
                    }
                    return;
                }
                // the upstream hasn't stopped yet but we don't have a value available
                if (empty) {
                    break;
                }

                child.onNext(t);
                emission++;
            }

            // if we are at a request boundary, a terminal event can be still emitted without requests
            if (emission == requests) {
                if (child.isUnsubscribed()) {
                    return;
                }
```

```java
            boolean stop = done;   // order matters here!
            boolean empty = queue.isEmpty();
            
            // if no more values, emit an error or completion event
            if (stop && empty) {
                Throwable ex = error;
                if (ex != null) {
                    child.onError(ex);
                } else {
                    child.onCompleted();
                }
                return;
            }
        }
        
        // decrement the current request amount by the emission count
        if (emission != 0L && requests != Long.MAX_VALUE) {
            BackpressureUtils.produced(requested, emission);
        }
        
        // indicate that we have performed the outstanding amount of work
        missed = counter.addAndGet(-missed);
        if (missed == 0) {
            return;
        }
        // if a concurrent getAndIncrement() happened, we loop back and continue
    }
}
```

Creating source operators

One creates a source operator by implementing the `OnSubscribe` interface and then calls `Observable.create` with it:

```java
OnSubscribe<T> onSubscribe = (Subscriber<? super T> child) -> {
    // logic here
};

Observable<T> observable = Observable.create(onSubscribe);
```

Note: a common mistake when writing an operator is that one simply calls onNext disregarding backpressure; one should use `fromCallable` instead for synchronously (blockingly) generating a single value.

The `logic here` could be arbitrary complex logic. Usually, one creates a class implementing `Subscription` and `Producer`, sets it on the `child` and works out the emission pattern:

```java
OnSubscribe<T> onSubscribe = (Subscriber<? super T> child) -> {
    MySubscription mys = new MySubscription(child, otherParams);
    child.add(mys);
    child.setProducer(mys);
    
    mys.runBusinessLogic();
};
```

Converting a callback-API to reactive

One of the reasons custom sources are created is when one converts a classical, callback-based 'reactive' API to RxJava. In this case, one has to setup the callback on the non-RxJava source and wire up unsubscription if possible:

```
OnSubscribe<Data> onSubscribe = (Subscriber<? super Data> child) -> {
    Callback cb = event -> {
        if (event.isSuccess()) {
            child.setProducer(new SingleProducer<Data>(child, event.getData()));
        } else {
            child.onError(event.getError());
        }
    };

    Closeable c = api.query("someinput", cb);

    child.add(Subscriptions.create(() -> Closeables.closeQuietly(c)));
};
```

In this example, the `api` takes a callback and returns a `Closeable`. Our handler signals the data by setting a `SingleProducer` of it to deal with downstream backpressure. If the downstream wants to cancel a running API call, the wrap to `Subscription` will close the query.

However, in case the callback is called more than once, one has to deal with backpressure a different way. At this level, perhaps the most easiest way is to apply `onBackpressureBuffer` or `onBackpressureDrop` on the created `Observable`:

```
OnSubscribe<Data> onSubscribe = (Subscriber<? super Data> child) -> {
    Callback cb = event -> {
        if (event.isSuccess()) {
            child.onNext(event.getData());
        } else {
            child.onError(event.getError());
        }
    };

    Closeable c = api.query("someinput", cb);

    child.add(Subscriptions.create(() -> Closeables.closeQuietly(c)));
};

Observable<T> observable = Observable.create(onSubscribe).onBackpressureBuffer();
```

Creating intermediate operators

Writing an intermediate operator is more difficult because one may need to coordinate request amount between the upstream and downstream.

Intermediate operators are nothing but Subscribers themselves, wrapping the downstream Subscriber themselves, modulating the calls to onXxxmethods and they get subscribed to the upstream's Observable:

```
Func1<T, R> mapper = ...

Observable<T> source = ...

OnSubscribe<R> onSubscribe = (Subscriber<? super R> child) -> {

    source.subscribe(new MapSubscriber<T, R>(child) {
        @Override
        public void onNext(T t) {
            child.onNext(function.call(t));
        }

        // ... etc
    });

}
```

Depending on whether the safety-net of the Observable.subscribe method is too much of an overhead, one can call Observable.unsafeSubscribe but then the operator has to manage and unsubscribe its own resources manually.

This approach has a common pattern that can be factored out - at the expense of more allocation and indirection - and became the lift operator.

The lift operator takes an Observable.Operator<R, T> interface implementor where R is the output type towards the downstream and T is the input type from the upstream. In our example, we can rewrite the operator as follows:

```
Operator<R, T> op = child ->
    return new MapSubscriber<T, R>(child) {
        @Override
        public void onNext(T t) {
            child.onNext(function.call(t));
        }

        // ... etc
    };
}

source.lift(op)...
```

The constructor of Subscriber(Subscriber<?>) has some caveats: it shares the underlying resource management between child and MapSubscriber. This has the unfortunate effect that when the business logic calls MapSubscriber.unsubscribe, it may inadvertently unsubscribe the child's resources prematurely. In addition, it sets up the Subscriber in a way that calls to setProducer are forwarded to the child as well. Sometimes it is acceptable, but generally one should avoid this coupling by implementing these custom Subscribers among the following pattern:

```
public final class MapSubscriber<T, R> extends Subscriber<T> {
    final Subscriber<? super R> child;

    final Function<T, R> mapper;
```

```java
    public MapSubscriber(Subscriber<? super R> child, Func1<T, R> mapper) {
        // no call to super(child) !
        this.child = child;
        this.mapper = mapper;

        // prevent premature requesting
        this.request(0);
    }

    // setup the unsubscription and request links to downstream
    void init() {
        child.add(this);
        child.setProducer(n -> requestMore(n));
    }

    @Override
    public void onNext(T t) {
        try {
            child.onNext(mapper.call(t));
        } catch (Throwable ex) {
            Exceptions.throwIfFatal(ex);
            // if something crashed non-fatally, unsubscribe from upstream and signal the error
            unsubscribe();
            onError(ex);
        }
    }

    @Override
    public void onError(Throwable e) {
        child.onError(e);
    }

    @Override
    public void onCompleted() {
        child.onCompleted();
    }

    void requestMore(long n) {
        // deal with the downstream requests
        this.request(n);
    }
}

Operator<R, T> op = child -> {
    MapSubscriber<T, R> parent = new MapSubscriber<T, R>(child, mapper);
    parent.init();
    return parent;
}
```

Some operators may not emit the received value to the `child` subscriber (such as filter). In this case, one has to call `request(1)` to ask for a replenishment because the downstream doesn't know about the dropped value and won't request itself:

```java
// ...

    @Override
    public void onNext(T t) {
        try {
```

```
            if (predicate.call(t)) {
                child.onNext(t);
            } else {
                request(1);
            }
        } catch (Throwable ex) {
            Exceptions.throwIfFatal(ex);
            unsubscribe();
            onError(ex);
        }
    }
}
// ...
```

When an operator maps an `onNext` emission to a terminal event then before calling the terminal event it should unsubscribe the subscriber to upstream (usually called the parent). In addition, because upstream may (legally) do something like this:
```
child.onNext(blah);
//  no check for unsubscribed here
child.onCompleted();
```

we should ensure that the operator complies with the `Observable` contract and only emits one terminal event so we use a defensive done flag:
```
boolean done; // = false;

@Override
public void onError(Throwable e) {
    if (done) {
        return;
    }
    done = true;
    ...
}

@Override
public void onCompleted(Throwable e) {
    if (done) {
        return;
    }
    done = true;
    ...
}
```

An example of this pattern is seen in `OnSubscribeMap`.

Java 9 features with examples

Java is a general purpose, high-level programming language developed by Sun Microsystems. It is concurrent, class-based, object-oriented, and specifically designed to have as few implementation dependencies as possible. Java was meant to follow the "Write Once Run Anywhere" (WORA) principle, i.e., Java is meant to be platform independent.

To learn more about the Java programming language in details, click here.

Like any other software, Java also comes with many different versions as it develops and gets improved, with new features getting added in every major upgrade.
Java 9 was a major upgrade from Java 8 that has brought us a lot of features for developers. Java 9 was released on July 27, 2019. In this article, we will look into Java 9 features in detail:

1. Improved Javadoc

Java 9 update came with an updated Java documentation. We no longer need to use Google to find the right documentation. The new Javadoc came with search right in the API documentation itself. Moreover, the Javadoc output was HTML5 compliant. Every Javadoc page includes information on which JDK module the class or interface comes from.

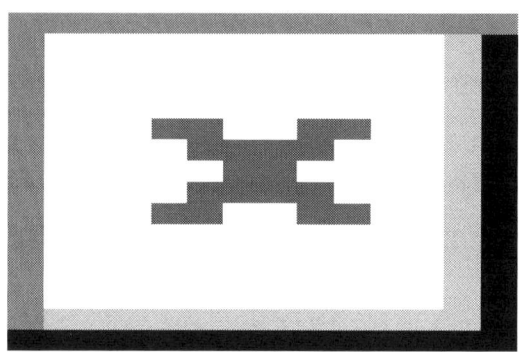

2. Factory methods for collections(like List, Map, Set and Map.Entry):

Many a times, you want to create a collection (e.g., a List or Set) in your Java program and fill it with some elements. That leads to repetitive coding where you instantiate the collection, followed by several 'add' calls. With Java 9, several so-called collection factory methods have been added.
List and Set interfaces have "of()" methods to create an empty or no-empty Immutable List or Set objects as shown below:
Empty List example:
```
List immutableList = List.of();
```

Non-Empty List example:
```
List immutableList = List.of("one", "two", "three");
```

Map has two set of methods: of() methods and ofEntries() methods to create an Immutable Map object and an Immutable Map.Entry object respectively.

Empty Map Example:

```
jshell> Map emptyImmutableMap = Map.of()
emptyImmutableMap ==> {}
```

Non-Empty Map Example:
```
jshell> Map nonemptyImmutableMap = Map.of(1, "one", 2, "two", 3, "three")
nonemptyImmutableMap ==> {2=two, 3=three, 1=one}
```

3. JShell: the interactive Java REPL

Oracle Corp. has introduced a new tool called "jshell". It stands for Java Shell and also known as REPL (Read Evaluate Print Loop). Many languages already feature an interactive Read-Eval-Print-Loop, and Java now joins this club. It is used to execute and test any Java Constructs like class, interface, enum, object, statements etc. very easily. You can launch jshell from the console and directly start typing and executing Java code. The immediate feedback of jshell makes it a great tool to explore APIs and try out language features.

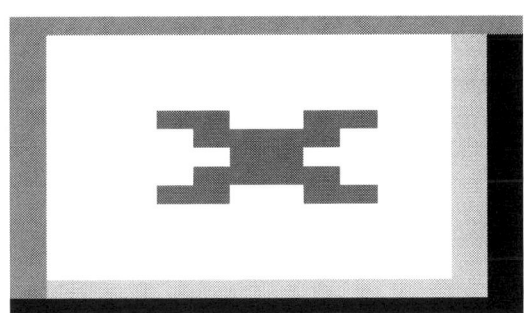

4. Stream API Improvements:

In Java SE 9, Oracle Corp. has added four useful new methods to java.util.Stream interface. As Stream is an interface, all those new implemented methods are default methods. It allows you to create declarative pipelines of transformations on collections. There are four new methods added to the Stream interface: dropWhile, takeWhile, ofNullable. The iterate method gets a new overload, allowing you to provide a Predicate on when to stop iterating.

5. Private methods in Interfaces:

In Java 8, we can provide method implementation in Interfaces using Default and Static methods. However we cannot create private methods in Interfaces. To avoid redundant code and more re-usability, Oracle Corp. introduced private methods in Java SE 9 Interfaces. From Java SE 9 on-wards, we can write private and private static methods too in an interface using 'private' keyword.

```java
public interface Card{

  private Long createCardID(){
    // Method implementation goes here.
  }


  private static void displayCardDetails(){
    // Method implementation goes here.
  }


}
```

6. Multi-Resolution Image API:

In Java SE 9, Oracle Corp. introduced a new Multi-Resolution Image API. Important interface in this API is MultiResolutionImage . It is available in java.awt.image package. MultiResolutionImage encapsulates a set of images with different Height and Widths and allows us to query them with our requirements.

7. The Java(9) Platform module system:

One of the big changes or java 9 feature is the Module System. Oracle Corp. introduced the following features as part of Jigsaw Project:

- Modular JDK
- Modular Java Source Code
- Modular Run-time Images
- Encapsulate Java Internal APIs
- Java Platform Module System

Before Java SE 9 versions, we are using Monolithic Jars to develop Java-Based applications. This architecture has lot of limitations and drawbacks. To avoid all these shortcomings, Java SE 9 comes with the Module System.

8. Improvements in Process API:

Java SE 9 is coming with some improvements in Process API. They have added couple new classes and methods to ease the controlling and managing of OS processes.
Two new interfcase in Process API:

- java.lang.ProcessHandle
- java.lang.ProcessHandle.Info

9. HTTP/2 Client

A new way of performing HTTP calls arrives with Java 9. As existing or Legacy HTTP Client API has numerous issues (like supports HTTP/1.1 protocol and does not support HTTP/2 protocol and WebSocket, works only in Blocking mode and lot of performance issues.), they are replacing this HttpURLConnection API with new HTTP client. They are going to introduce new HTTP 2 Client API under "java.net.http" package. It supports both HTTP/1.1 and HTTP/2 protocols. It supports both Synchronous (Blocking Mode) and Asynchronous Modes. It supports Asynchronous Mode using WebSocket API.

```
HttpClient client = HttpClient.newHttpClient();

HttpRequest req =
   HttpRequest.newBuilder(URI.create("http://www.google.com"))
            .header("User-Agent", "Java")
            .GET()
            .build();




HttpResponse resp = client.send(req, HttpResponse.BodyHandler.asString());
```

10. Miscellaneous Java 9 Features:

- GC (Garbage Collector) Improvements
- Stack-Walking API
- Filter Incoming Serialization Data
- Deprecate the Applet API
- Indify String Concatenation
- Enhanced Method Handles
- Java Platform Logging API and Service
- Compact Strings
- Parser API for Nashorn
- Javadoc Search

P.S.: Java SE 9 has reached end of support. Users of Java SE 9 should switch to Java SE 10 or later.

The release of Java 9 and Java 9 features is a milestone in the Java ecosystem. The modular framework developed under Project Jigsaw will be part of this Java SE release and major features in this are the JShell (REPL tool), important API changes and JVM-level changes to improve the performance and debuggability of the JVM.

Before we unravel the Java 9 features in detail let us take a peek at previous Java versions and see what were the shortcomings and how Java 9 helped to overcome those anomalies:-

- The Java Standard Edition platform and the JDK were not navigable for small computing devices
- There was no overall security and maintenance of JDK
- There was no overall improvement in application performance
- It was difficult for Java developers to build and uphold the code libraries and larger applications, for both the Java SE and EE Platforms

Watch The Course Preview

In this blog post I will categorize Java 9 features in the following manner:

1. Process API updates in Java 9
2. HTTP/2 client in Java 9
3. Java Shell Scripting (Read-Eval-Print-Loop) in Java 9
4. Multi-release JAR files feature in Java 9
5. More Concurrency Updates feature in Java 9
6. Project Jigsaw in Java 9

What is new in Java 9?

I have picked a few new Java 9 features, which I feel are worth knowing about. Let's see what are these features:-

Process API updates in Java 9

Java's Process API has been quite primitive, with support only to launch new processes, redirect the processes' output, and error streams. In this release, the updates to the Process API enable the following:

- Getting the PID of the current JVM process and any other processes spawned by the JVM
- Enumerate the processes running in the system to get information such as PID, name, and resource usage
- Managing process trees
- Managing subprocesses

Let's look at a sample code, which prints the current PID as well as the current process information:

```
1   public class NewFeatures{
2
3       public static void main(String [] args) {
4
5           ProcessHandle currentProcess = ProcessHandle.current();
6
7           System.out.println("PID:"+ currentProcess.getPid());
8
9           ProcessHandle.Info currentProcessInfo = currentProcess.info();
10
11          System.out.println("Info:" + currentProcessInfo);
12      }
```

HTTP/2 client in Java 9

This Java 9 feature is expected to change in the subsequent releases and may even be removed completely.

Earlier Developers often resort to using third-party libraries, such as Apache HTTP, Jersey, and so on. In addition to this, Java's HTTP API predates the HTTP/1.1 specification and is synchronous and hard to maintain. These limitations called for the need to add a new API. The new HTTP client API provides the following:

- A simple and concise API to deal with most HTTP requests
- Support for HTTP/2 specification
- Better performance
- Better security
- A few more enhancements

Let's see a sample code to make an HTTP GET request using the new APIs. Below

```
1  module newfeatures{
2      requires jdk.incubator.httpclient;
3  }
```

is the module definition defined in the file module-info.java:

The following code uses the HTTP Client API, which is part

```
1
2  import jdk.incubator.http.*;
3  import java.net.URI;
4  public class Http2Feature{
5      public static void main(String[] args) throws Exception{
6          HttpClient client = HttpClient.newBuilder().build();
7          HttpRequest request = HttpRequest
   .newBuilder(new URI(http://httpbin.org/get;))
8  .GET()
9  .version(HttpClient.Version.HTTP_1_1)
10 .build();
11 HttpResponse.String response = client.send(request,
   HttpResponse.BodyHandler.asString());
12 System.out.println("Status code:" + response.statusCode());</pre>
13 <pre>System.out.println("Response Body:" + response.body());
14     }
15 }
16
17
```

of jdk.incubator.httpclient module:

Trending Courses in this category

Java Shell Scripting (Read-Eval-Print-Loop) in Java 9

You must have seen languages, such as Ruby, Scala, Groovy, Clojure, and others shipping with a tool, which is often called **REPL (Read-Eval-Print-Loop)**. This REPL tool is extremely useful in trying out the language features. For example, in Scala, we can write a simple Hello World program as **scala>println("Hello World");**

Some of the advantages of the **JShell REPL** are as follows:

- Experienced developers can quickly prototype and experiment before adopting it in their main code base
- Java developers can now boast of a REPL

Let's run the JShell command, as shown in the following image:

```
root@ubuntu-512mb-blr1-01:~# jshell
|  Welcome to JShell -- Version 9-ea
|  For an introduction type: /help intro

jshell> "Hello World"
$1 ==> "Hello World"

jshell>
```

Multi-release JAR files feature in Java 9

As of now, JAR files can contain classes that can only run on the Java version they were compiled for. To leverage the new features of the Java platform on newer versions, the library developers have to release a newer version of their library. Soon, there will be multiple versions of the library being maintained by the developers, which can be a nightmare. To overcome this limitation, these Java 9 features of multi-release JAR files allows developers to build JAR files with different versions of class files for different Java versions. The following example makes it more clear.

Here is an illustration of the current JAR files:

```
jar root

 - A.class

 - B.class

 - C.class
```

Here is how multi-release JAR files look:

```
jar root

    - A.class

    - B.class

    - C.class

    - META-INF

        - versions

            - 9

                - A.class

            - 10

                - B.class
```

In the preceding illustration, the JAR files support class files for two Java versions–9 and 10.

So, when the earlier JAR is executed on Java 9, the A.class under the versions – 9 folders are picked up for execution.

On a platform that doesn't support multi-release JAR files, the classes under the versions directory are never used. So,if you run the multi-release JAR file on Java 8, it's as good as running a simple JAR file.

More Concurrency Updates feature in Java 9

In this update, a new class, **java.util.concurrent.Flow** has been introduced, which has nested interfaces supporting the implementation of a publish-subscribe framework. The publish-subscribe framework enables developers to build components that can asynchronously consume a live stream of data by setting up publishers that produce the data and subscribers that consume the data via subscription, which manages them. The four new interfaces are as follows:

- java.util.concurrent.Flow.Publisher
- java.util.concurrent.Flow.Subscriber
- java.util.concurrent.Flow.Subscription
- java.util.concurrent.Flow.Processor (which acts as both Publisher and Subscriber).

Project Jigsaw in Java 9

The main aim of this project is to introduce the concept of **modularity**; **support** for creating modules in Java 9 and then apply the same to the **JDK**; that is, **modularize the JDK**.

Some of the **benefits** of **modularity** are as follows:

- **Strong encapsulation**: The modules can access only those parts of the module that have been made available for use. So, the public classes in a package are not public unless the package is explicitly exported in the module info file.
- **Clear Dependencies**: Modules must declare which other modules they would be using via the requires clause.
- Combining modules to create a smaller runtime, which can be easily scaled to smaller computing devices.
- **Reliable**: Applications are more reliable by eliminating **run-time errors**. **Example:-** you must have experienced your application failing during run-time due to missing classes, resulting in **ClassNotFoundException**.

There are various **JEPs**, which are part of this project, as follows:

- **JEP 200 – modular JDK**: This applies the Java platform module system to modularize the JDK into a set of modules that can be combined at compile time, build time, or runtime.
- **JEP 201 – modular source code**: This modularizes the JDK source code into modules and enhances the build tools to compile the modules.
- **JEP 220 – modular runtime images**: This restructures the JDK and JRE runtime images to accommodate modules and to improve performance, security, and maintainability.
- **JEP 260 – encapsulate most internal APIs**: This allows a lot of internal APIs to be accessed directly or via reflection. Accessing internal APIs that are bound to change is quite risky. To prevent its use, they are being encapsulated into modules and only those internal APIs that are widely used are being made available until a proper API is in its place.
- **JEP 261 – module system**: This implements the module system Java specification by changing the Java programming language, JVM, and other standard APIs
- **JEP 282: jlink, the Java linker**: This allows packaging modules and their dependencies into smaller run times.

So, this was all about Java 9 and new Java 9 features.

Java 10 is finally here! A closer look at the new features

Oracle delivers the new Java 10 just in time with the previously announced deadline. Those who expected big and groundbreaking changes will be disappointed, but there are still a lot of great new features. Falk Sippach, trainer, software developer and project manager at OIO Orientation at Objects GmbH, took a good look at those and will go here into further detail.

Java 10 is final – Is it that time again?

Imagine if the latest version of Java was released on time and on schedule according to the official release date. It'll never happen, you say? Well, apparently it just did. We even have proof! (And more here.) It does seem a bit awkward, because it feels like Java 9 was only just released. But, just as it was announced back in early September 2017, the next version has been released on its planned deadline.

The development of new Java versions was, up until now, very feature driven. This meant that you had to wait for a few years for the next release. Major changes like Generics, Lambdas, Streams, and Jigsaw made this fact bearable, but quite a lot of the smaller and very useful language improvements were consistently delayed this way. Oracle has now switched to a new, time based model – a move that is still being discussed and viewed as controversial.

We as Java developers can now look forward to a new version every six months. But apparently, not everyone agrees with this proceeding and the Java Community is split on the issue. Larger companies also appreciated the stability and the low rate of change of Java so far.

Oracle has responded to these concerns and continues to offer long-term releases on a regular basis, but also at longer intervals. And after Java 8, it is Java 11, which will probably receive a long term support again.

Java 9 and Java 10 on the other hand will only be supported for the time period of half a year, until the next release is due. In fact, Java 9's support has just ended, since Java 10 is out. You can find more information on this on Oracle Support Roadmap.

Honestly, one reason why this hasn't been too bad is because we all had barely acclimated to Java 9 yet. Quite a lot of tool and framework manufacturers are still working on adapting to the new module system. For instance, JUnit has just released version 5.1, which supports testing in Jigsaw modules. Even the world of Java Enterprise (Java EE, EE4J, Jakarta EE and MicroProfile) seems to be unsure how modularization is supposed to find its way into application servers and servlets containers.

Java 10 – The new features

But let's get back to Java 10. Thanks to the short time frame you don't have to struggle through too long release notes. The list on the OpenJDK project page is quite clearly laid out:

List of Java 10 features

From a developer's point of view, the Java Enhancement Process (JEP) 286 for the **Local Variable Type Inference** is most interesting feature on this list. Type Inference is the conclusion on data types from the remaining specifications of the code and the typing rules. This prevents an unnecessary inflation of the source code and saves time on the writing work, which increases the readability in return. We already know this fairly well, since it mimics the same structure from Java and its Lambda parameters and with the Diamond operator for generic data containers respectively for anonymous, inner classes.

```
1   // Type inference bei Parametern von Lambda Ausdrücken (Java 8)
2   Function<String, String> helloFunction = s -> "Hello " + s;
3
4   // Inference of generics (Diamond Operator, since Java 7)
5   List strings = new ArrayList<>();
6   strings.add(helloFunction.apply("World"));
7
8   // Inference of generics (Diamond Operator) with anonymous inner
9   classes (Java 9 -> JEP 213)
10  Consumer printer = new Consumer<>() {
11      @Override
12      public void accept(String string) {
13          System.out.println(string);
```

```
14     }
15   };
     strings.forEach(printer::accept);
```

With the keyword var, local variables can now be defined very concisely and their data type results directly from the assignment of the value. While the Diamond operator concludes the Type information from the left side of the assignment, the Local-Variable Type Inference is exactly the other way around.

```
1  // int
2  var zahl = 5;
3  // String
4  var string = "Hello World";
5  // BigDecimal
6  var objekt = BigDecimal.ONE;
```

Once declared var, variables are set to the assigned data type. If you want to assign values of other types later, you will get compiler errors due to the failed type conversion.

```
1  // Type is set by the compiler at declaration and initial
   allocations
2  var zahl = 5;
3  zahl = 7L; // Incompatible types: possible lossy conversion from
   long to int
4
5  var objekt = BigDecimal.ONE;
6  objekt = BigInteger.TEN; // Incompatible types: BigInteger cannot
   be converted to BigDecimal
```

This means that a value must always be assigned during declaration. Otherwise, compiler errors will also occur even if a value is guaranteed to be assigned shortly afterwards, as in the following example.

```
1  // Declaration of "var" only at direct initialization of the
2  variable
3  var flag = true;
4  var number; // Compiler error
5  if (flag) {
6      number = 5;
7  } else {
```

```
8        number = 7;
    }
```

The type inference also works with generic types and within the foreach loop. However, the combination with the Diamond operator leads to a container of object references, due to the missing type information and thus leads to less type security.

```
1   // Inference at reallocation of a value (var does not imply "final")
2   var zahl = 5;
3   zahl = 7;
4
5   // Inference is also usable with "final", otherwise "effectively
    final semantic" applies since Java 8
6   final var zahl = 5;
```

Variables declared with var, as the name already indicates, are not automatically unchangeable. You can combine them with the keyword final. They are also effectively final (if there is only one assignment) and can therefore also be used from inner classes and lambda expressions without explicitly declaring them as final.

```
1   // Inference of generic types (List<String>)
2   var strings = Arrays.asList("World", "Java 10");
3
4   // Inference in Loops
5   for (var string : strings) {
6       System.out.println("Hello " + string);
7   }
8
9   // In combination with the Diamond Operator this leads to the
10  inference of List<Object>
11  var strings = new ArrayList<>();
12  strings.add("Hello World");
13  for (var string : strings) {
14      System.out.println(string.replace("World", "Java 10")); // cannot
15  find symbol 'replace'
16  }
17
18  var strings2 = new ArrayList<String>();
```

```
19  strings2.add("Hello World");
20  for (var string : strings2) {
        System.out.println(string.replace("World", "Java 10"));
    }
```

The type inference uses the concrete type, what means that for anonymous internal classes, two instances derived from the same interface may not be assigned to the same var variable.

```
1   // Inference uses exact typing
2   var runnable = new Runnable() {
3       @Override
4       public void run() {
5       }
6   };
7   // incompatible types: <anonymous Runnable> cannot be converted to
    <anonymous Runnable>
8   runnable = new Runnable() {
9       @Override
10      public void run() {
11      }
12  };
```

However, this also means that newly implemented methods can be called without compiler errors for local types (anonymous inner class implementations) (reverseMe()).

```
1   // Inference of local types
2   var myReversibleStringList = new ArrayList<String>() {
3       List<String> reverseMe() {
```

```
4          var reversed = new ArrayList<String>(this);
5          Collections.reverse(reversed);
6          return reversed;
7      }
8  };
9  myReversibleStringList.add("World");
10 myReversibleStringList.add("Hello");
11
12 System.out.println(myReversibleStringList.reverseMe());
```

Work is still ongoing for Java 11, specifically on an extension of the local variable Type Inference, which works in lambda expressions. This is necessary for combining type inferences with type annotations.

The remainder of the release notes are concerned with the infrastructural area and the operation of Java applications. The **G1**, which has been the standard garbage collector since Java 9, can parallelize the full garbage collection and thus shorten the stop-the-world cycles. The memory footprint can be reduced by sharing loaded classes between multiple Java applications.

Furthermore, there is a new, still-experimental **JIT** (Just-In-Time) **Compiler** (Graal) and improvements to the JVM for working with Docker Containers. The OpenJDK Trust Store is now delivered with a certain amount of root certificates, which was previously only available for Oracle Java SE versions.

The class-library (JDK) has also gone through some small changes as well. This includes an overloaded version of orElseThrow() in the Optional class and various factory methods for creating unmodifiable collections and stream collectors. Further changes can be found in the release notes or via the JDK-API-Diff tool.

Java 10 is the fastest release of a java version in its 23 year history. Java has been criticized for its slow growth and evolution, but Java 10 just shattered that concept. Java 10 is a release with many futuristic changes, the scope and impact of which may not be obvious but are far fetching.

In this article we will discuss the various features added in Java10 release. Before that, let's go over some changes introduced to java release model.

Table of Contents [hide]
- 0.1 Long Term Support Model

- 0.2 Oracle JDK vs Open JDK
- 1 Java 10 Features
    - 1.1 Time-Based Release Versioning (JEP 322)
    - 1.2 Local-Variable Type Inference (JEP 286)
    - 1.3 Experimental Java-Based JIT Compiler (JEP 317)
    - 1.4 Application Class-Data Sharing (JEP 310)
    - 1.5 Parallel Full GC for G1 (JEP 307)
    - 1.6 Garbage-Collector Interface (JEP 304)
    - 1.7 Additional Unicode Language-Tag Extensions (JEP 314)
    - 1.8 Root Certificates (JEP 319)
    - 1.9 Thread-Local Handshakes (JEP 312)
    - 1.10 Heap Allocation on Alternative Memory Devices (JEP 316)
    - 1.11 Remove the Native-Header Generation Tool – javah (JEP 313)
    - 1.12 Consolidate the JDK Forest into a Single Repository (JEP 296)
    - 1.13 API Changes2 Conclusion

Long Term Support Model

Starting 2017, Oracle & the Java community announced its shift to a new 6 month cadence for Java. It moved to a Long Term Support (LTS) model for Oracle Java SE products.

What does this mean?

LTS version of the products will offer premier and sustained support from Oracle and it will be targeted every 3 years.

Each Java release is modelled after one or two major feature, these features drives the release. Any obstacle, postpones the release and late to market. Project Jigsaw was a major feature of Java 9, it pushed out the release dates a couple of times and the release was delayed by more than 1.5 years. 6 months cadence release will follow a release train. Release train will have a schedule every 6 months. Features which make the cut get boarded on the train; else they wait for the next scheduled train.

Oracle JDK vs Open JDK

In order to be more developer friendly, Oracle & Java community now promotes the OpenJDK binaries as primary JDK going forward. This is big relief from earlier days, where the JDK binaries were propriety and licensed by Oracle, which had various restrictions around redistribution. Oracle will however keep producing their JDK, but only for long term support releases. This is a move towards being more cloud & container friendly, as the open JDK binaries can be distributed as part of a container.

What does this mean?

Open JDK binaries will be released every 6 months, while Oracle JDK binaries will be releases every 3 years (LTS version).

Which JDK binaries will be adopted?

Large organizations take time to move between the versions; they cling on to the version until they can. Industry adoption for Java 6 was more than Java 7 and then Industry is gradually moving to Java 8. In my opinion LTS version will be most favoured ones by the enterprises. However, whether it would be the LTS version of Oracle JDK or the Open JDK is yet to known, partly because there's lot going on the cloud space.

Java 9 & 10 are non-LTS release. Java 11 which is due in September 2018 will be a LTS release.

Java 10 Features

Let's take a sneak peak of the features available in Java 10.

1. Time-Based Release Versioning (JEP 322)

With adoption of time based release cycle, Oracle changed the version-string scheme of the Java SE Platform and the JDK, and related versioning information, for present and future time-based release models.

The new pattern of the Version number is:

$FEATURE: counter will be incremented every 6 months and will be based on feature release versions, e.g: JDK 10, JDK 11.

$INTERIM: counter will be incremented for non-feature releases that contain compatible bug fixes and enhancements but no incompatible changes. Usually this will be zero, as there will be no interim release in a six month period. This kept for future revision to the release model.

$UPDATE: counter will be incremented for compatible update releases that fix security issues, regressions, and bugs in newer features. This is updated one month after the feature release and every 3 months thereafter. The April 2018 release is JDK 10.0.1, the July release is JDK 10.0.2, and so forth

$PATCH: counter will be incremented for an emergency release to fix a critical issue.
New API's have been added to get these counter values programmatically. Let's take a look;

Now, let us take a look at Java launcher which returns the version information:

The version number format is "10" as there's no other counter which is other than zero. The date of release is added. 18.3 can be read as Year 2018 & 3rd Month, build 10+46 is 46th build for version 10. For a hypothetical build 93 of JDK 10.0.1, the build will be 10.0.1+93

2. Local-Variable Type Inference (JEP 286)

Local-Variable Type Inference is the biggest new feature in Java 10 for developers. It adds type inference to declarations of local variables with initializers. Local type inference can be used only in the following scenarios:

- Limited only to Local Variable with initializer
- Indexes of enhanced for loop or indexes
- Local declared in for loop

```
for (var i = 0; i < numbers.size(); i++) {
  System.out.println(numbers.get(i));
```

Experimental Java-Based JIT Compiler (JEP 317)

This feature enables the Java-based JIT compiler, Graal, to be used as an experimental JIT compiler on the Linux/x64 platform. This is by far the most futuristic inclusion in the Java 10 feature list.

Graal was introduced in Java 9. It's an alternative to the JIT compiler which we have been used to. It's a plugin to the JVM, which means that the JIT compiler is not tied to JVM and it can be dynamically plugged in and replaced with any another plugin which JVMCI compliant (Java-Level JVM Compiler Interface). It also brings Ahead of Time (AOT) compilation in java world. It also supports polyglot language interpretation.

"A Java based Just in Time Compiler written in Java to convert the java bytecode to machine code." Is it confusing? If JVM is written in Java, then don't you need a JVM to run the JVM? The JVM can be compiled AOT and then JIT compiler can be used within JVM it for enhancing performance through live code optimization.

Graal is a complete rewrite of the JIT compiler in Java from scratch. Previous JIT complier was written in c++. It's considered one for the final stage of evolution for any programming language.

You can switch to Graal with following jvm parameters:

```
-XX:+UnlockExperimentalVMOptions -XX:+UseJVMCICompiler
```
You can learn more about Graal from Chris Seaton presentation.

Application Class-Data Sharing (JEP 310)

This feature helps in improving the startup footprint, extends the existing Class-Data Sharing ("CDS") feature to allow application classes to be placed in the shared archive.

JVM while starting performs some preliminary steps, one of which is loading classes in memory. If there are several jars having multiple classes, then the lag in the first request is clearly visible. This becomes an issue with serverless architecture, where boot time is critical. In order to bring down application startup time, Application class-data sharing can be used. The idea is to reduce footprint by sharing common class metadata across different Java processes. This can be achieved by the following 3 steps:

Determining the classes to archive: Use the java launcher to create a list of files to archive, this can be achieved by the following parameters:

```
$java -Xshare:off -XX:+UseAppCDS -XX:DumpLoadedClassList=hello.lst -cp hello.jar HelloWorld
```
Creating the AppCDS archive: Use java launcher to create the archive of the list of files to be used for Application CDS, this can be achieved by following parameters:

```
$java -Xshare:dump -XX:+UseAppCDS -XX:SharedClassListFile=hello.lst -XX:SharedArchiveFile=hello.jsa -cp hello.jar
```
Using the AppCDS archive: Use Java launcher with the following parameters to use Application CDS.

```
$java -Xshare:on -XX:+UseAppCDS -
XX:SharedArchiveFile=hello.jsa -cp hello.jar HelloWorld
```

Parallel Full GC for G1 (JEP 307)

G1 garbage collector was made default in JDK 9. G1 Garbage collector avoids any full garbage collection, but when concurrent threads for collection cannot revive the memory fast enough users experience is impacted.

This change improves the G1 worst-case latency by making the full GC parallel. The mark-sweep-compact algorithm from G1 collector is parallelized as part of this change and will be triggered when concurrent threads for collection can't revive the memory fast enough.

Garbage-Collector Interface (JEP 304)

This JEP is futuristic change. It improves the code isolation of different garbage collectors by introducing a common Garbage Collector Interface.

This change provides better modularity to the Internal GC Code. It will help in the future for adding new GC without changing existing codebase, also help in removing or housekeeping of the previous GC.

Additional Unicode Language-Tag Extensions (JEP 314)

This feature enhances java.util.Locale and related APIs to implement additional Unicode extensions of BCP 47 language tags. As of Java SE 9, the supported BCP 47 U language-tag extensions are – ca and nu. This JEP will add support for the following additional extensions:

- cu (currency type)
- fw (first day of week)
- rg (region override)
- tz (time zone)

In order to support these additional extensions, changes are made to various APIs to provide information based on U or additional extensions.

```
java.text.DateFormat::get*Instance
java.text.DateFormatSymbols::getInstance
java.text.DecimalFormatSymbols::getInstance
java.text.NumberFormat::get*Instance
java.time.format.DateTimeFormatter::localizedBy
java.time.format.DateTimeFormatterBuilder::getLocalizedDat
eTimePattern
```

```
java.time.format.DecimalStyle::of
java.time.temporal.WeekFields::of
java.util.Calendar::{getFirstDayOfWeek,getMinimalDaysInWee
k}
java.util.Currency::getInstance
java.util.Locale::getDisplayName
java.util.spi.LocaleNameProvider
```

Root Certificates (JEP 319)

In order to promote OpenJDK and make it more appealing to community users, this feature provides a default set of root Certification Authority (CA) certificates in the JDK. This will also mean that both Oracle & Open JDK binaries will be functionally the same.

Critical security components such as TLS will work by default in OpenJDK builds going forward.

Thread-Local Handshakes (JEP 312)

This is an internal JVM feature to improve performance.

A handshake operation is a callback that is executed for each JavaThread while that thread is in a safepoint safe state. The callback is executed either by the thread itself or by the VM thread while keeping the thread in a blocked state.

This feature provides a way to execute a callback on threads without performing a global VM safepoint. Make it both possible and cheap to stop individual threads and not just all threads or none.

Heap Allocation on Alternative Memory Devices (JEP 316)

Applications have become memory hungry, there's an increase in cloud-native applications, in-memory databases, streaming applications. In order to cater to these services, there are various memory architectures available. This feature enhances the capability of HotSpot VM to allocate the Java object heap on an alternative memory device, such as an NV-DIMM, specified by the user.

This JEP targets alternative memory devices that have the same semantics as DRAM, including the semantics of atomic operations, and can, therefore, be used instead of DRAM for the object heap without any change to existing application code.

Remove the Native-Header Generation Tool – javah (JEP 313)

This is a housekeeping change to remove javah tool from JDK. The tool functionality is added in   as part of JDK 8, which provides ability to write native header files at the compile time rendering   useless.

Consolidate the JDK Forest into a Single Repository (JEP 296)

Over the years there have been various Mercurial repositories in for JDK codebase. Different repositories do provide some advantage, but it also had various operational downsides. As part of this change, numerous repositories of the JDK forest are combined into a single repository in order to simplify and streamline development.

API Changes

Java 10 has added and removed (Yes It's not a Typo) API's.

Java 9 introduced enhanced deprecation where certain API's were marked to be removed in future releases.

API's Removed: You can find the API's removed

http://cr.openjdk.java.net/~iris/se/10/latestSpec/#APIs-removed

API's Added: 73 new API's was added in Java 10. You can find the API's added along with comparison

JSR 383: Java SE 10

Java™ Platform, Standard Edition
API Differences between Java SE 9 (build 181) & Java SE 10 (build 44)
Compiled by Iris Clark

Specification Statistics

			Changed	Added	Removed	Unchanged	Total
Date Created	2018-02-20 21:04:51						
Old Version	Java™ SE 9 (build 181)	Documents 576	0	0		4360	**4936**
New Version	Java™ SE 10 (build 44)	Contexts 1314	73	10		53377	**54774**

Processed Packages 236

Specification Detail

(*) Columns: (1) - Changed, (2) - Added, (3) - Removed, ∑ - Total

Package	Documents						Contexts					
	Modified				Unchanged	Total	Modified				Unchanged	Total
	1	2	3	∑			1	2	3	∑		
java.applet				0	6	**6**				0	54	**54**
java.awt	6			6	156	**162**	11	1		12	3195	**3207**
java.awt.color				0	8	**8**				0	206	**206**
java.awt.datatransfer				0	13	**13**				0	109	**109**
java.awt.desktop				0	31	**31**				0	76	**76**
java.awt.dnd				0	25	**25**				0	249	**249**
java.awt.doc-files				0	4	**4**				0	4	**4**
java.awt.event	1			1	44	**45**	1			1	572	**573**
java.awt.font				0	21	**21**				0	436	**436**
java.awt.geom	3			3	34	**37**	3			3	744	**747**
java.awt.im	1			1	4	**5**	1			1	46	**47**
java.awt.im.spi				0	4	**4**				0	29	**29**
java.awt.image	2			2	54	**56**	3			3	922	**925**
java.awt.image.renderable				0	8	**8**				0	109	**109**
java.awt.print				0	11	**11**				0	85	**85**
java.beans				0	42	**42**				0	324	**324**
java.beans.beancontext	1			1	23	**24**	1			1	211	**212**
java.io	8			8	78	**86**	12	8		20	943	**963**
java.lang	13			13	106	**119**	33	6	10	49	2016	**2065**
java.lang.annotation				0	13	**13**				0	47	**47**
java.lang.doc-files				0	2	**2**				0	2	**2**
java.lang.instrument				0	7	**7**				0	35	**35**

java.lang.invoke	8	8	12	**20**	18	1	**19**	274	**293**
java.lang.management	3	3	18	**21**	3	3	**6**	187	**193**
java.lang.module	2	2	18	**20**	2		**2**	162	**164**
java.lang.ref		0	8	**8**			**0**	28	**28**
java.lang.reflect	2	2	29	**31**	2	1	**3**	278	**281**
java.math	1	1	4	**5**	1		**1**	177	**178**
java.net	11	11	55	**66**	18	2	**20**	795	**815**
java.net.doc-files		0	1	**1**			**0**	1	**1**
java.net.spi		0	2	**2**			**0**	3	**3**
java.nio	1	1	14	**15**	1		**1**	321	**322**
java.nio.channels	4	4	53	**57**	5	2	**7**	318	**325**
java.nio.channels.spi		0	7	**7**			**0**	52	**52**
java.nio.charset	1	1	12	**13**	1		**1**	114	**115**
java.nio.charset.spi		0	2	**2**			**0**	5	**5**
java.nio.file	3	3	45	**48**	5	1	**6**	282	**288**
java.nio.file.attribute	1	1	25	**26**	1		**1**	145	**146**
java.nio.file.spi		0	3	**3**			**0**	34	**34**
java.rmi		0	21	**21**			**0**	64	**64**
java.rmi.activation		0	17	**17**			**0**	100	**100**
java.rmi.dgc		0	4	**4**			**0**	14	**14**
java.rmi.registry		0	4	**4**			**0**	19	**19**
java.rmi.server		0	28	**28**			**0**	154	**154**
java.security	9	9	85	**94**	53		**53**	679	**732**
java.security.acl	9	9	0	**9**	39		**39**	0	**39**
java.security.cert		0	55	**55**			**0**	475	**475**
java.security.interfaces	1	1	13	**14**	2		**2**	47	**49**

java.security.spec			0	29	**29**		0	154	**154**
java.sql			0	56	**56**		0	1300	**1300**
java.text	9		9	22	**31**	24	24	494	**518**
java.text.spi			0	7	**7**		0	27	**27**
java.time	2		2	17	**19**	2	2	798	**800**
java.time.chrono	3		3	19	**22**	3	3	413	**416**
java.time.format	3		3	6	**9**	6	1	7	139	**146**
java.time.temporal	1		1	16	**17**	2		2	188	**190**
java.time.zone			0	7	**7**			0	72	**72**
java.util	35		35	96	**131**	112	21	133	2089	**2222**
java.util.concurrent	24		24	49	**73**	43	1	44	1137	**1181**
java.util.concurrent.atomic	2		2	15	**17**	2		2	334	**336**
java.util.concurrent.locks	4		4	11	**15**	7	4	11	204	**215**
java.util.doc-files	1		1	3	**4**	1		1	3	**4**
java.util.function			0	44	**44**			0	122	**122**
java.util.jar	2		2	10	**12**	3	2	5	292	**297**
java.util.logging			0	18	**18**			0	218	**218**
java.util.prefs			0	10	**10**			0	119	**119**
java.util.regex	1		1	4	**5**	3		3	74	**77**
java.util.spi	4		4	7	**11**	4	2	6	37	**43**
java.util.stream	5		5	9	**14**	7	4	11	265	**276**
java.util.zip	3		3	19	**22**	8		8	401	**409**
javax.accessibility			0	29	**29**			0	378	**378**
javax.activation			0	18	**18**			0	140	**140**
javax.activity			0	4	**4**			0	16	**16**
javax.annotation			0	7	**7**			0	22	**22**

javax.annotation.processing			0	14	**14**		0	62	**62**
javax.crypto	4		4	21	**25**	7	7	231	**238**
javax.crypto.interfaces			0	5	**5**		0	14	**14**
javax.crypto.spec			0	17	**17**		0	98	**98**
javax.imageio	1		1	11	**12**	1	1	345	**346**
javax.imageio.event			0	6	**6**		0	30	**30**
javax.imageio.metadata			0	7	**7**		0	203	**203**
javax.imageio.metadata.doc-files	1		1	6	**7**	1	1	6	**7**
javax.imageio.plugins.bmp			0	2	**2**		0	6	**6**
javax.imageio.plugins.jpeg			0	5	**5**		0	41	**41**
javax.imageio.plugins.tiff	1		1	12	**13**	5	5	484	**489**
javax.imageio.spi	3		3	9	**12**	3	3	114	**117**
javax.imageio.stream			0	12	**12**		0	221	**221**
javax.jws			0	8	**8**		0	33	**33**
javax.jws.soap			0	8	**8**		0	31	**31**
javax.lang.model	1		1	3	**4**	5	1	6	22	**28**
javax.lang.model.element	3		3	26	**29**	5	5	186	**191**
javax.lang.model.type			0	19	**19**		0	86	**86**
javax.lang.model.util	26		26	15	**41**	104	2	106	164	**270**
javax.management	3		3	71	**74**	3	3	579	**582**
javax.management.loading	1		1	7	**8**	1	1	61	**62**
javax.management.modelmbean	1		1	12	**13**	1	1	137	**138**
javax.management.monitor	1		1	10	**11**	1	1	160	**161**
javax.management.openmbean	1		1	25	**26**	1	1	253	**254**
javax.management.relation	1		1	27	**28**	1	1	264	**265**
javax.management.remote	1		1	18	**19**	1	1	106	**107**

javax.management.remote.rmi	3	3	8	**11**	3	2	5	157	**162**
javax.management.timer		0	4	**4**			0	63	**63**
javax.naming		0	42	**42**			0	352	**352**
javax.naming.directory		0	19	**19**			0	194	**194**
javax.naming.event		0	8	**8**			0	43	**43**
javax.naming.ldap		0	23	**23**			0	154	**154**
javax.naming.spi		0	13	**13**			0	48	**48**
javax.net		0	3	**3**			0	16	**16**
javax.net.ssl	4	4	40	**44**	5		5	353	**358**
javax.print	24	24	2	**26**	83		83	111	**194**
javax.print.attribute	20	20	7	**27**	115		115	55	**170**
javax.print.attribute.standard	72	72	4	**76**	283		283	449	**732**
javax.print.event	6	6	3	**9**	14		14	27	**41**
javax.rmi		0	2	**2**			0	8	**8**
javax.rmi.CORBA		0	10	**10**			0	71	**71**
javax.rmi.ssl		0	3	**3**			0	16	**16**
javax.script	1	1	12	**13**	1		1	146	**147**
javax.security.auth	2	2	8	**10**	7		7	47	**54**
javax.security.auth.callback		0	11	**11**			0	72	**72**
javax.security.auth.kerberos		0	9	**9**			0	106	**106**
javax.security.auth.login		0	16	**16**			0	65	**65**
javax.security.auth.spi		0	2	**2**			0	7	**7**
javax.security.auth.x500		0	3	**3**			0	24	**24**
javax.security.cert		0	8	**8**			0	40	**40**
javax.security.sasl		0	11	**11**			0	68	**68**
javax.sound.midi	7	7	22	**29**	11		11	289	**300**

javax.sound.midi.spi			0	5	**5**		0	27	**27**
javax.sound.sampled	13		13	22	**35**	24	24	275	**299**
javax.sound.sampled.spi			0	5	**5**		0	34	**34**
javax.sql			0	20	**20**		0	218	**218**
javax.sql.rowset			0	13	**13**		0	298	**298**
javax.sql.rowset.serial			0	11	**11**		0	146	**146**
javax.sql.rowset.spi			0	9	**9**		0	65	**65**
javax.swing	7		7	237	**244**	6	1	7	4709	**4716**
javax.swing.border			0	12	**12**		0	170	**170**
javax.swing.colorchooser			0	5	**5**		0	37	**37**
javax.swing.doc-files			0	0	**0**		0	0	**0**
javax.swing.event	1		1	49	**50**	1	1	258	**259**
javax.swing.filechooser			0	5	**5**		0	46	**46**
javax.swing.plaf			0	50	**50**		0	218	**218**
javax.swing.plaf.basic	2		2	192	**194**	1	1	2	2343	**2345**
javax.swing.plaf.metal	3		3	68	**71**	3	3	677	**680**
javax.swing.plaf.multi			0	32	**32**		0	508	**508**
javax.swing.plaf.multi.doc-files	1		1	0	**1**	1	1	0	**1**
javax.swing.plaf.nimbus			0	7	**7**		0	63	**63**
javax.swing.plaf.nimbus.doc-files			0	1	**1**		0	1	**1**
javax.swing.plaf.synth			0	52	**52**		0	855	**855**
javax.swing.plaf.synth.doc-files			0	2	**2**		0	2	**2**
javax.swing.table			0	16	**16**		0	310	**310**
javax.swing.text	3		3	114	**117**	3	3	1588	**1591**
javax.swing.text.doc-files			0	0	**0**		0	0	**0**
javax.swing.text.html			0	45	**45**		0	622	**622**

javax.swing.text.html.parser		0	11	**11**		0	188	**188**
javax.swing.text.rtf		0	2	**2**		0	8	**8**
javax.swing.tree	1	1	20	**21**	1	1	419	**420**
javax.swing.undo		0	10	**10**		0	109	**109**
javax.swing.undo.doc-files		0	0	**0**		0	0	**0**
javax.tools	1	1	24	**25**	1	1	200	**201**
javax.transaction		0	4	**4**		0	10	**10**
javax.transaction.xa	1	1	3	**4**	2	2	57	**59**
javax.xml	1	1	1	**2**	2	2	16	**18**
javax.xml.bind	1	1	31	**32**	1	1	307	**308**
javax.xml.bind.annotation	2	2	39	**41**	2	2	120	**122**
javax.xml.bind.annotation.adapters		0	8	**8**		0	26	**26**
javax.xml.bind.attachment		0	3	**3**		0	12	**12**
javax.xml.bind.helpers		0	9	**9**		0	111	**111**
javax.xml.bind.util		0	4	**4**		0	14	**14**
javax.xml.catalog		0	8	**8**		0	34	**34**
javax.xml.crypto		0	16	**16**		0	85	**85**
javax.xml.crypto.dom		0	4	**4**		0	26	**26**
javax.xml.crypto.dsig		0	19	**19**		0	137	**137**
javax.xml.crypto.dsig.dom		0	3	**3**		0	15	**15**
javax.xml.crypto.dsig.keyinfo		0	9	**9**		0	49	**49**
javax.xml.crypto.dsig.spec		0	12	**12**		0	35	**35**
javax.xml.datatype	1	1	6	**7**	1	1	142	**143**
javax.xml.namespace	3	3	0	**3**	4	4	12	**16**
javax.xml.parsers		0	7	**7**		0	91	**91**
javax.xml.soap	7	7	21	**28**	10	10	268	**278**

javax.xml.stream	3	3	13	**16**	3	3	237	**240**
javax.xml.stream.events		0	15	**15**		0	74	**74**
javax.xml.stream.util		0	5	**5**		0	71	**71**
javax.xml.transform		0	13	**13**		0	98	**98**
javax.xml.transform.dom		0	4	**4**		0	26	**26**
javax.xml.transform.sax	1	1	5	**6**	1	1	42	**43**
javax.xml.transform.stax		0	3	**3**		0	18	**18**
javax.xml.transform.stream		0	3	**3**		0	34	**34**
javax.xml.validation		0	8	**8**		0	64	**64**
javax.xml.ws		0	33	**33**		0	180	**180**
javax.xml.ws.handler		0	8	**8**		0	40	**40**
javax.xml.ws.handler.soap		0	3	**3**		0	8	**8**
javax.xml.ws.http		0	3	**3**		0	6	**6**
javax.xml.ws.soap		0	8	**8**		0	47	**47**
javax.xml.ws.spi		0	5	**5**		0	43	**43**
javax.xml.ws.spi.http		0	4	**4**		0	38	**38**
javax.xml.ws.wsaddressing	1	1	2	**3**	1	1	17	**18**
javax.xml.xpath	1	1	14	**15**	1	1	86	**87**
org.ietf.jgss		0	9	**9**		0	159	**159**
org.omg.CORBA	1	1	192	**193**	1	1	1502	**1503**
org.omg.CORBA.DynAnyPackage		0	5	**5**		0	13	**13**
org.omg.CORBA.ORBPackage		0	4	**4**		0	15	**15**
org.omg.CORBA.TypeCodePackage		0	5	**5**		0	23	**23**
org.omg.CORBA.doc-files	1	1	1	**2**	1	1	1	**2**
org.omg.CORBA.portable		0	21	**21**		0	169	**169**
org.omg.CORBA_2_3		0	2	**2**		0	8	**8**

org.omg.CORBA_2_3.portable		0	5	**5**		0	23	**23**
org.omg.CosNaming	7	7	28	**35**	7	7	231	**238**
org.omg.CosNaming.NamingContextExtPackage	3	3	4	**7**	3	3	40	**43**
org.omg.CosNaming.NamingContextPackage	15	15	4	**19**	15	15	107	**122**
org.omg.Dynamic	1	1	1	**2**	1	1	5	**6**
org.omg.DynamicAny	9	9	41	**50**	9	9	744	**753**
org.omg.DynamicAny.DynAnyFactoryPackage	2	2	1	**3**	2	2	10	**12**
org.omg.DynamicAny.DynAnyPackage	4	4	1	**5**	4	4	19	**23**
org.omg.IOP	26	26	13	**39**	26	26	160	**186**
org.omg.IOP.CodecFactoryPackage	2	2	1	**3**	2	2	10	**12**
org.omg.IOP.CodecPackage	6	6	1	**7**	6	6	28	**34**
org.omg.Messaging	1	1	2	**3**	1	1	10	**11**
org.omg.PortableInterceptor	23	23	36	**59**	23	23	249	**272**
org.omg.PortableInterceptor.ORBInitInfoPackage	4	4	2	**6**	4	4	29	**33**
org.omg.PortableServer	9	9	46	**55**	9	9	235	**244**
org.omg.PortableServer.CurrentPackage	2	2	1	**3**	2	2	10	**12**
org.omg.PortableServer.POAManagerPackage	2	2	2	**4**	2	2	22	**24**
org.omg.PortableServer.POAPackage	20	20	1	**21**	20	20	93	**113**
org.omg.PortableServer.ServantLocatorPackage		0	2	**2**		0	8	**8**
org.omg.PortableServer.portable		0	2	**2**		0	10	**10**
org.omg.SendingContext		0	3	**3**		0	3	**3**
org.omg.stub.java.rmi		0	2	**2**		0	4	**4**
org.w3c.dom	1	1	29	**30**	1	1	254	**255**
org.w3c.dom.bootstrap		0	2	**2**		0	7	**7**

org.w3c.dom.events			0	9	9		0	53	53
org.w3c.dom.ls	1		1	11	12	1	1	81	82
org.w3c.dom.ranges			0	4	4		0	37	37
org.w3c.dom.traversal			0	5	5		0	44	44
org.w3c.dom.views			0	3	3		0	5	5
org.xml.sax	2		2	16	18	2	2	137	139
org.xml.sax.ext			0	9	9		0	64	64
org.xml.sax.helpers	2		2	9	11	4	4	169	173
Total	576	0	576	4360	**4936**	1314	73107	53377	**54774**

© 2018 Oracle Corporation and/or its affiliates

Let's go through a few additions:

- List, Map & Set Interfaces are added with a static copyOf(Collection) method. Its returns an unmodifiable List, Map or Set containing the entries provided. For a List, if the given List is subsequently modified, the returned List will not reflect such modifications.
- Optional & its primitive variations get a method orElseThrow(). This is exactly same as get(), however the java doc states that it is a preferred alternative then get()
- Collectors class gets various methods for collecting unmodifiable collections (Set, List, Map)

Copy

```
                    new
    add "Jack Nicholson"
    add "Marlon Brando"
    out                    // prints [Jack Nicholson,
Marlon Brando]
// New API added - Creates an UnModifiable List from a
List.

    out                         // prints [Jack
Nicholson, Marlon Brando]
// copyOfActors.add("Robert De Niro"); Will generate an
// UnsupportedOperationException
```

```
        add "Robert De Niro"
        out                     // prints [Jack Nicholson,
Marlon Brando, Robert De Niro]
        out                     // prints [Jack
Nicholson, Marlon Brando]

        " "

    // New API added - is preferred option then get() method
                    // same as name.get()

    // New API added - Collectors.toUnmodifiableList


    // collect.add("Tom Hanks"); // Will generate an
    // UnsupportedOperationException
```

Java 10: New Features And Enhancements

Oracle has recently delivered the new Java 10 within the previously announced deadline. It is a feature release of the Java SE platform which got released on March 20, 2018. It contains various new features and enhancements into many functional areas. Some of its key improvements include enhancements for garbage collection and compilation as well as local variable types.

Georges Saab, vice president of Software Development in Oracle's Java Platform Group, said that "Oracle is committed to rapidly evolving and delivering new innovations in the Java platform – this being the first in our newly adopted release cycle and licensing model. We're especially proud of the simplicity of this release, which introduces useful new features, removes unnecessary elements, and is easy for developers to use."

Read Also: 5 Things You Need to Know About Java 9

Java 10 is scheduled to be a short-term release and its public updates are slated to end in six months. Moreover, the JDK 11 will be the long-term support (LTS) version of Java which is due in September.

Let's take a sneak peek into what new features are in Java 10.

These features are defined through the JDK Enhancement Proposals (JEP) process and are mentioned below:

– **Application Data-Class Sharing:**

This JEP extends the existing Class-Data Sharing ("CDS") feature for allowing application classes to be placed in the shared archive in order to improve startup and footprint.

– **Parallel Full GC for G1:**

It improves G1 worst-case latencies by making the full GC parallel.

– **Garbage Collector Interface:**

It will improve the source code isolation of different garbage collectors by introducing a clean garbage collector (GC) interface.

– **Consolidate the JDK Forest into a Single Repository:**

It will combine the numerous repositories of the JDK forest into a single repository to simplify and streamline development.

– **Local-Variable Type Inference:**

It will enhance the Java Language to extend type inference to declarations of local variables with initializers and also introduces var to Java, something that is common in other languages.

– **Remove the Native-Header Generator Tool:**

It will remove the javah tool from the JDK since it has been superseded by superior functionality in javac.

– **Thread-Local Handshakes:**

It introduces a way to execute a callback on threads without performing a global VM safepoint. Makes it both possible and cheap to stop individual threads and not just all threads or none.

– **Time-Based Release Versioning:**

It revises the version-string scheme of the Java SE Platform and the JDK, and related versioning information, for present and future time-based release models.

– **Root Certificates:**

It provides a default set of root Certification Authority (CA) certificates in the JDK.

– **Heap Allocation on Alternative Memory Devices:**

It enables the HotSpot VM to allocate the Java object heap on an alternative memory device, such as an NV-DIMM, specified by the user.

– **Experimental Java-Based JIT Compiler:**

It enables the Java-based JIT compiler, Graal, to be used as an experimental JIT compiler on the Linux/x64 platform.

– **Additional Unicode Language-Tag Extensions:**

It will enhance the java.util.Locale and related APIs to implement additional Unicode extensions of BCP 47 language tags.

Removed Features and Options in Java 10

This will describe the APIs, features, and options that were removed in Java SE 10 and JDK 10. It may also identify potential compatibility issues that you could encounter when migrating to JDK 10.

Deprecated Features and Options in Java 10

This will describe the deprecated APIs, features, and options that have been identified as deprecated in this release and are subject to removal from future versions of Java SE and the JDK. They should be used with that possibility in mind.

Image Source: Oracle

So overall, it seems that Java 10 is not exactly a cause for alarm as it doesn't contain any major changes or improvements. However, it represents the first release in the new, more frequent and gradual release cycle. It's impressive enough that Java 10 was delivered as-promised and Just-in-Time like its compiler. The coming time will tell "Will Java community accept the new delivered model". For developers, it is much more useful than its previous versions.

We haven't fully immersed ourselves in Java 10 yet, and Java 11 is here. Java 11 is important for more than just a few reasons. Oracle has revamped its support model and come up with a release train that'll bring rapid updates, about every 6 months.

They've changed the licensing and support model which means if you download the Java 11 Oracle JDK, it will be paid for commercial use.

Does that mean that I need to pay for Java from now on?
NO. Not necessarily unless you download the Oracle JDK and use it in production.

Note: IntelliJ IDEA 2018.2.4 Community Edition already has support for Java 11.

Table of Contents [hide]
- 1 Why is Java 11 important?
- 2 Which JDK build should I download and what are the benefits of each of them?
- 3 How to download Java 11 Free Version?
- 4 Java 11 Features
  - 4.1 Running Java File with single command
  - 4.2 Java String Methods
  - 4.3 Local-Variable Syntax for Lambda Parameters
  - 4.4 Nested Based Access Control
  - 4.5 JEP 309: Dynamic Class-File Constants
  - 4.6 JEP 318: Epsilon: A No-Op Garbage Collector
  - 4.7 JEP 320: Remove the Java EE and CORBA Modules
  - 4.8 JEP 328: Flight Recorder
  - 4.9 JEP 321: HTTP Client
  - 4.10 Reading/Writing Strings to and from the Files
  - 4.11 JEP 329: ChaCha20 and Poly1305 Cryptographic Algorithms

- 4.12 JEP 315: Improve Aarch64 Intrinsics
- 4.13 JEP 333: ZGC: A Scalable Low-Latency Garbage Collector (Experimental)
- 4.14 JEP 335: Deprecate the Nashorn JavaScript Engine

Why is Java 11 important?

Java 11 is the second LTS release after Java 8. Since Java 11, Oracle JDK would no longer be free for commercial use.

You can use it in developing stages but to use it commercially, you need to buy a license. If you don't, you can get an invoice bill from Oracle any day!

Java 10 was the last free Oracle JDK that could be downloaded.

Oracle stops Java 8 support from January 2019. You'll need to pay for more support. You can continue using it, but won't get any patches/security updates.

Oracle will not be providing free long-term support (LTS) for any single Java version since Java 11.

While Oracle JDK is no longer free, you can always download the Open JDK builds from Oracle or other providers such as AdoptOpenJDK, Azul, IBM, Red Hat etc. In my opinion, unless you are looking for Enterprise level usage with the appetite to pay for the support fees, you can use OpenJDK and upgrade them as and when necessary.

Which JDK build should I download and what are the benefits of each of them?

Since Oracle has created a release train in which a new version would come up every six months, if you are using the free Open JDK by Oracle, you will need to update it every six months, since Oracle won't provide free updates once the new version is released. This can be challenging to adapt to a company.

Pay for commercial support to Oracle and migrate only from one LTS version to the next LTS version.
This way you'll get all the updates and support for Java 11 till 2026. You can download Java 17 in 2022.

Stay on free Java version even after its support ends. Though you won't get security updates and it can open up security loopholes.

Oracle won't provide commercial support or updates for Java 9 and Java 10. You need to look for other alternative builds in order to keep using them for free.

Having understood the baggage Java 11 comes with, lets now analyze the important features in Java 11 for developers. We'll discuss some important JEPs too.

Note: JavaFX will be available as a separate module and not tied to Java JDK's 6-month release cycle schedule.

Java 11 Features

Let's discuss the new features introduced with Java 11 from the JEP Process.

Java 11 Features

Running Java File with single command

One major change is that you don't need to compile the java source file
with `javac` tool first. You can directly run the file with **java** command and it implicitly compiles.
This feature comes under JEP 330.

Following is a sneak peek at the new methods of Java String class introduced in Java 11:

Java String Methods

isBlank() – This instance method returns a boolean value. Empty Strings and Strings with only white spaces are treated as blank.

```
import java.util.*;

public class Main {
    public static void main(String[] args) throws Exception {
        // Your code here!

        System.out.println(" ".isBlank()); //true

        String s = "Anupam";
        System.out.println(s.isBlank()); //false
        String s1 = "";
        System.out.println(s1.isBlank()); //true
    }
}
```

lines()

This method returns a string array which is a collection of all substrings split by lines.

```
import java.util.stream.Collectors;

public class Main {
    public static void main(String[] args) throws Exception {

        String str = "JD\nJD\nJD";
        System.out.println(str);

System.out.println(str.lines().collect(Collectors.toList()));
    }
}
```

The output of the above code is:

Output Input Comments 0

```
JD
JD
JD
[JD, JD, JD]
```

strip(), stripLeading(), stripTrailing()

`strip()` – Removes the white space from both, beginning and the end of string.

> **But we already have trim(). Then what's the need of strip()?**
> `strip()` is "Unicode-aware" evolution of `trim()`.
>
> When `trim()` was introduced, Unicode wasn't evolved. Now, the new strip() removes all kinds of whitespaces leading and trailing(check the method `Character.isWhitespace(c)` to know if a unicode is whitespace or not)

An example using the above three methods is given below:

```
public class Main {
    public static void main(String[] args) throws Exception {
        // Your code here!

        String str = " JD ";
        System.out.print("Start");
        System.out.print(str.strip());
        System.out.println("End");

        System.out.print("Start");
```

```
            System.out.print(str.stripLeading());
            System.out.println("End");

            System.out.print("Start");
            System.out.print(str.stripTrailing());
            System.out.println("End");
    }
```

The output in the console from the above code is:

```
Output  Input  Comments  0

StartJDEnd
StartJD End
Start  JDEnd
```

repeat(int)

The repeat method simply repeats the string that many numbers of times as mentioned in the method in the form of an int.

```
public class Main {
    public static void main(String[] args) throws Exception {
        // Your code here!

        String str = "=".repeat(2);
        System.out.println(str);  //prints ==
    }
}
```

Local-Variable Syntax for Lambda Parameters

JEP 323, Local-Variable Syntax for Lambda Parameters is the only language feature release in Java 11.
In Java 10, Local Variable Type Inference was introduced. Thus we could infer the type of the variable from the RHS – `var list = new ArrayList<String>();`

JEP 323 allows `var` to be used to declare the formal parameters of an implicitly typed lambda expression.

We can now define :

```
(var s1, var s2) -> s1 + s2
```
This was possible in Java 8 too but got removed in Java 10. Now it's back in Java 11 to keep things uniform.

But why is this needed when we can just skip the type in the lambda?
If you need to apply an annotation just as @Nullable, you cannot do that without defining the type.

Limitation of this feature – You must specify the type var on all parameters or none.
Things like the following are not possible:

```
(var s1, s2) -> s1 + s2 //no skipping allowed
(var s1, String y) -> s1 + y //no mixing allowed

var s1 -> s1 //not allowed. Need parentheses if you use var in lambda.
```

Nested Based Access Control

Before Java 11 this was possible:

```
public class Main {

    public void myPublic() {
    }

    private void myPrivate() {
    }

    class Nested {

        public void nestedPublic() {
            myPrivate();
        }
    }
}
```

private method of the main class is accessible from the above-nested class in the above manner.
But if we use Java Reflection, it will give an `IllegalStateException`.

```
Method method = ob.getClass().getDeclaredMethod("myPrivate");
method.invoke(ob);
```

Java 11 nested access control addresses this concern in reflection.
`java.lang.Class` introduces three methods in the reflection
API: `getNestHost()`, `getNestMembers()`, and `isNestmateOf()`.

JEP 309: Dynamic Class-File Constants

The Java class-file format now extends support a new constant pool form, CONSTANT_Dynamic. The goal of this JEP is to reduce the cost and disruption of developing new forms of materializable class-file constraints, by creating a single new constant-pool form that can be parameterized with user-provided behavior. This enhances performance

JEP 318: Epsilon: A No-Op Garbage Collector

Unlike the JVM GC which is responsible for allocating memory and releasing it, Epsilon only allocates memory.
It allocates memory for the following things:

- Performance testing.
- Memory pressure testing.
- VM interface testing.
- Extremely short lived jobs.
- Last-drop latency improvements.
- Last-drop throughput improvements.

Now Elipson is good only for test environments. It will lead to OutOfMemoryError in production and crash the applications.

The benefit of Elipson is no memory clearance overhead. Hence it'll give an accurate test result of performance and we can no longer GC for stopping it.

Note: This is an experimental feature.

JEP 320: Remove the Java EE and CORBA Modules

The modules were already deprecated in Java 9. They are now completely removed.

Following packages are removed: ,   ,   ,   ,
                       ,   ,   ,

JEP 328: Flight Recorder

Flight Recorder which earlier used to be a commercial add-on in Oracle JDK is now open sourced since Oracle JDK is itself not free anymore.

JFR is a profiling tool used to gather diagnostics and profiling data from a running Java application.
Its performance overhead is negligible and that's usually below 1%. Hence it can be used in production applications.

JEP 321: HTTP Client

Java 11 standardizes the Http CLient API.
The new API supports both HTTP/1.1 and HTTP/2. It is designed to improve the overall performance of sending requests by a client and receiving responses from the server. It also natively supports WebSockets.

Reading/Writing Strings to and from the Files

Java 11 strives to make reading and writing of String convenient.
It has introduced the following methods for reading and writing to/from the files:

- readString()
- writeString()

Following code showcases an example of this

```
Path path = Files.writeString(Files.createTempFile("test",
".txt"), "This was posted on JD");
System.out.println(path);
String s = Files.readString(path);
System.out.println(s); //This was posted on JD
```

JEP 329: ChaCha20 and Poly1305 Cryptographic Algorithms

Java 11 provides ChaCha20 and ChaCha20-Poly1305 Cipher implementations. These algorithms will be implemented in the SunJCE provider.

JEP 315: Improve Aarch64 Intrinsics

Improve the existing string and array intrinsics, and implement new intrinsics for the java.lang.Math sin, cos, and log functions, on AArch64 processors.

JEP 333: ZGC: A Scalable Low-Latency Garbage Collector (Experimental)

Java 11 has introduced a low latency GC. This is an experimental feature.
It's good to see that Oracle is giving importance to GC's.

JEP 335: Deprecate the Nashorn JavaScript Engine

Nashorn JavaScript script engine and APIs are deprecated thereby indicating that they will be removed in the subsequent releases.

90 New Features (and APIs) in JDK 11

The new six-month release cadence of the JDK means before we've even really figured out what the new features are in JDK 10, along comes JDK 11. I posted an earlier blog where I listed all 109 new features and APIs I could find in JDK 10, so it seemed obvious to do the same thing for JDK 11. I'm going to use a different format to the previous post. In this post, I'll divide things two sections: features that are visible to developers and everything else. This way if you're interested in just what will affect your development work you can skip the second part.

The total I counted was 90 (that's JEPs plus new classes and methods, excluding the individual ones for the HTTP client and Flight Recorder). Although that's eleven less than I found in JDK 10, I think it's fair to say more functionality has been added to JDK 11, certainly at the JVM level.

Developer Visible Features

JDK 11 is pretty light on things that change the way you code. There is one small change to the language syntax, a fair number of new APIs and the ability to run single-file applications without the need to use the compiler. Also, visible is the removal of the java.se.ee aggregator module, which may impact migrating an existing application to JDK 11.

JEP 323: Local-Variable Syntax for Lambda Parameters

JDK 10 introduced Local-Variable Type Inference (JEP 286). This simplifies code, as you no longer need to explicitly state the type of a local-variable but can, instead, use var. JEP 323 extends the use of this syntax to the parameters of Lambda expressions. Here's a simple example:

```
list.stream()
      .map((var s) -> s.toLowerCase())
      .collect(Collectors.toList());
```

Of course, the astute Java programmer would point out that Lambda expressions already have type inference so the use of var would (in this case) be superfluous. We could just as easily write the same code as:

```
list.stream()
       .map(s -> s.toLowerCase())
       .collect(Collectors.toList());
```

Why add var support, then? The answer is for one special case, which is when you want to add an annotation to the Lambda parameter. It is not possible to do this without a type being involved. To avoid having to use the explicit type we can use var to simplify things, thus:

```
list.stream()
      .map((@Notnull var s) -> s.toLowerCase())
      .collect(Collectors.toList());
```

This feature has required changes to the Java Language Specification (JLS), specifically:

- Page 24: The description of the *var* special identifier.
- Page 627-30: Lambda parameters
- Page 636: Runtime evaluation of Lambda expressions
- Page 746: Lambda syntax

JEP 330: Launch Single-File Source-Code Programs

One of the criticisms of Java is that it can be verbose in its syntax and the 'ceremony' associated with running even a trivial application can make it hard to approach as a beginner. To write an application that just prints "Hello World!" requires you to write a class with a public static void main method and use the System.out.println method. Having done this, you must then compile the code using javac. Finally, you can run the application to be welcomed to the world. Doing the same thing in most scripting languages is *significantly* simpler and quicker.

JEP 330 eliminates the need to compile a single-file application, so now you can type

```
java HelloWorld.java
```

The java launcher will identify that the file contains Java source code and will compile the code to a class file before executing it.

Parameters placed *after* the name of the source file are passed as parameters when executing the application. Parameters placed *before* the name of the source file are passed as parameters to the java launcher after the code has been compiled (this allows for things like the classpath to be set on the command line). Parameters that are relevant to the compiler (such as the classpath) will also be passed to javac for compilation.

As an example:

```
java -classpath /home/foo/java Hello.java Bonjour
```

would be equivalent to:

```
javac -classpath /home/foo/java Hello.java
java -classpath /home/foo/java Hello Bonjour
```

This JEP also provides 'shebang' support. To reduce the need to even mention the java launcher on the command line, this can be included on the first line of the source file. For example:

```
#!/usr/bin/java --source 11
public class HelloWorld {

    ...
```

It is necessary to specify the —source flag with the version of Java to use.

JEP 321: HTTP Client (Standard)

JDK 9 introduced a new API to provide support for the HTTP Client protocol (JEP 110). Since JDK 9 introduced the Java Platform Module System (JPMS), this API was included as an *incubator module*. Incubator modules are intended to provide new APIs but without making them part of the Java SE standard. Developers can try the API and provide feedback. Once any necessary changes have been made (this API was updated in JDK 10), the API can be moved to become part of the standard.

The HTTP Client API is now part of the Java SE 11 standard. This introduces a new module and package to the JDK, java.net.http. The main types defined are

- HttpClient
- HttpRequest
- HttpResponse
- WebSocket

The API can be used synchronously or asynchronously. Asynchronous mode makes use of CompletableFutures and CompletionStages.

JEP 320: Remove The Java EE and CORBA Modules

With the introduction of JPMS in JDK 9, it was possible to divide the monolithic rt.jar file into multiple modules. An additional advantage of JPMS is it is now possible to create a Java runtime that only includes the modules you need for your application, reducing the size considerably. With cleanly defined module boundaries it is now simpler to remove parts of the Java API that are outdated. This is what this JEP does; the java.se.ee meta-module includes six modules that will no longer be part of the Java SE 11 standard and not included in the JDK. The affected modules are:

- corba
- transaction
- activation
- xml.bind
- xml.ws
- xml.ws.annotation

These modules have been deprecated since JDK 9 and were not included by default in either compilation or runtime. If you had tried compiling or running an application that used APIs from these modules on JDK 9 or JDK 10 they would have failed. If you use APIs from these modules in your code, you will need to supply them as a separate module or library. From asking audiences at my presentations, it seems that the java.xml modules, which are part of the JAX-WS, SOAP-based web services support are the ones that will cause most problems.

New APIs

A lot of the new APIs in JDK 11 result from the HTTP client module now being part of the standard, as well as the inclusion of Flight Recorder.

For a complete list of API changes, I refer the reader to the excellent comparison of different JDK versions produced by Gunnar Morling, which is available on Github.

What I list here are all the new methods other than those in the java.net.http and jdk.jfr modules. I've also not listed the new methods and classes in the java.security modules, which are pretty specific to the changes of JEP 324 and JEP 329 (there are six new classes and eight new methods).

java.io.ByteArrayOutputStream

- void writeBytes(byte[]): Write all the bytes of the parameter to the output stream

java.io.FileReader

Two new constructors that allow a Charset to be specified.

java.io.FileWriter

Four new constructors that allow a Charset to be specified.

java.io.InputStream

- io.InputStream nullInputStream(): Returns an InputStream that reads no bytes. When you first look at this method (and the ones in OutputStream, Reader and Writer), you wonder what use they are. You can think of them like /dev/null for throwing away output you don't need or providing an input that always returns zero bytes.

java.io.OutputStream

- io.OutputStream nullOutputStream()

java.io.Reader

- io.Reader nullReader()

java.io.Writer

- io.Writer nullWriter()

java.lang.Character

- String toString(int): This is an overloaded form of the existing method but takes an int instead of a char. The int is a Unicode code point.

java.lang.CharSequence

- int compare(CharSequence, CharSequence): Compares two CharSequence instances lexicographically. Returns a negative value, zero, or a positive value if the first sequence is lexicographically less than, equal to, or greater than the second, respectively.

java.lang.ref.Reference

- lang.Object clone(): I must admit, this one confuses me. The Reference class does not implement the Cloneable interface and this method will always throw a CloneNotSupportedException. There must be a reason for its inclusion, presumably for something in the future.

java.lang.Runtime
java.lang.System

No new methods here but worth mentioning that the runFinalizersOnExit() method has now been removed from both these classes (this could be a compatibility issue)

java.lang.String

I think this is one of the highlights of the new APIs in JDK 11. There are several useful new methods here.

- boolean isBlank(): Returns true if the string is empty or contains only white space codepoints, otherwise false.
- Stream lines(): Returns a stream of lines extracted from this string, separated by line terminators.
- String repeat(int): Returns a string whose value is the concatenation of this string repeated count times.
- String strip(): Returns a string whose value is this string, with all leading and trailing whitespace removed.
- String stripLeading(): Returns a string whose value is this string, with all leading whitespace removed.
- String stripTrailing(): Returns a string whose value is this string, with all trailing whitespace removed.

You probably look at strip() and ask, "How is this different to the existing trim() method?" The answer is that how whitespace is defined differs between the two.

java.lang.StringBuffer
java.lang.StringBuilder

Both these classes have a new compareTo() method that takes a StringBuffer/StringBuilder and returns an int. The lexographical comparison method is the same as the new compareTo() method of CharSequence.

java.lang.Thread

No additional methods but the destroy() and stop(Throwable) methods have been removed. The stop() method that takes no arguments is still present. This might present a compatibility issue.

java.nio.ByteBuffer
java.nio.CharBuffer
java.nio.DoubleBuffer
java.nio.FloatBuffer
java.nio.LongBuffer
java.nio.ShortBuffer

All these classes now have a mismatch() method that finds and returns the relative index of the first mismatch between this buffer and a given buffer.

java.nio.channels.SelectionKey

- int interestOpsAnd(int): Atomically sets this key's interest set to the bitwise intersection ("and") of the existing interest set and the given value.
- int interestOpsOr(int): Atomically sets this key's interest set to the bitwise union ("or") of the existing interest set and the given value.

java.nio.channels.Selector

- int select(java.util.function.Consumer, long): Selects and performs an action on the keys whose corresponding channels are ready for I/O operations. The long parameter is a timeout.
- int select(java.util.function.Consumer): As above, except without the timeout.
- int selectNow(java.util.function.Consumer): As above, except it is non-blocking.

java.nio.file.Files

- String readString(Path): Reads all content from a file into a string, decoding from bytes to characters using the UTF-8 charset.
- String readString(Path, Charset): As above, except decoding from bytes to characters using the specified Charset.
- Path writeString(Path, CharSequence, java.nio.file. OpenOption[]):Write a CharSequence to a file. Characters are encoded into bytes using the UTF-8 charset.
- Path writeString(Path, CharSequence, java.nio.file. Charset, OpenOption[]): As above, except Characters are encoded into bytes using the specified Charset.

java.nio.file.Path

- Path of(String, String[]): Returns a Path by converting a path string, or a sequence of strings that when joined form a path string.
- Path of(net.URI): Returns a Path by converting a URI.

java.util.Collection

- Object[] toArray(java.util.function.IntFunction): Returns an array containing all of the elements in this collection, using the provided generator function to allocate the returned array.

java.util.concurrent.PriorityBlockingQueue
java.util.PriorityQueue

- void forEach(java.util.function.Consumer): Performs the given action for each element of the Iterable until all elements have been processed or the action throws an exception.
- boolean removeAll(java.util.Collection): Removes all of this collection's elements that are also contained in the specified collection (optional operation).
- boolean removeIf(java.util.function.Predicate): Removes all of the elements of this collection that satisfy the given predicate.
- boolean retainAll(java.util.Collection): Retains only the elements in this collection that are contained in the specified collection (optional operation).

java.util.concurrent.TimeUnit

- long convert(java.time.Duration): Converts the given time duration to this unit.

java.util.function.Predicate

- Predicate not(Predicate). Returns a predicate that is the negation of the supplied predicate.

This is one of my favourite new APIs in JDK 11. As an example, you can convert this code:

```
lines.stream()
     .filter(s -> !s.isBlank())
```

to

```
lines.stream()
     .filter(Predicate.not(String::isBlank))
```

and if we use a static import it becomes:

```
lines.stream()
     .filter(not(String::isBlank))
```

Personally, I think this version is more readable and easier to understand.

java.util.Optional
java.util.OptionalInt
java.util.OptionalDouble
java.util.OptionalLong

- boolean isEmpty(): If a value is not present, returns true, otherwise false.

java.util.regex.Pattern

- Predicate asMatchPredicate(): I think this could be a hidden gem in the new JDK 11 APIs. Creates a predicate that tests if this pattern matches a given input string.

java.util.zip.Deflater

- int deflate(ByteBuffer): Compresses the input data and fills the specified buffer with compressed data.
- int deflate(ByteBuffer, int): Compresses the input data and fills the specified buffer with compressed data. Returns the actual number of bytes of data compressed.
- void setDictionary(ByteBuffer): Sets the preset dictionary for compression to the bytes in the given buffer. This is an overloaded form of an existing method that can now accept a ByteBuffer, rather than a byte array.
- void setInput(ByteBuffer): Sets input data for compression. Also an overloaded form of an existing method.

java.util.zip.Inflater

- int inflate(ByteBuffer): Uncompresses bytes into the specified buffer. Returns the actual number of bytes uncompressed.
- void setDictionary(ByteBuffer): Sets the preset dictionary to the bytes in the given buffer. An overloaded form of an existing method.
- void setInput(ByteBuffer): Sets input data for decompression. An overloaded form of an existing method.

javax.print.attribute.standard.DialogOwner

- This is a new class in JDK 11 and is an attribute class used to support requesting a print or page setup dialog be kept displayed on top of all windows or some specific window.

javax.swing.DefaultComboBoxModel
javax.swing.DefaultListModel

- void addAll(Collection): Adds all of the elements present in the collection.
- void addAll(int, Collection): Adds all of the elements present in the collection, starting from the specified index.

javax.swing.ListSelectionModel

- int[] getSelectedIndices(): Returns an array of all of the selected indices in the selection model, in increasing order.
- int getSelectedItemsCount(): Returns the number of selected items.

jdk.jshell.EvalException

- jshell.JShellException getCause(): Returns the wrapped cause of the throwable in the executing client represented by this EvalException or null if the cause is non-existent or unknown.

Non-Developer Features

JEP 181: Nest-Based Access Control

Java (and other languages) supports nested classes through inner classes. To make this work correctly requires the compiler to perform some tricks. Here's an example:

```java
public class Outer {
  private int outerInt;

    class Inner {
      public void printOuterInt() {
        System.out.println("Outer int = " + outerInt);
      }
    }
}
```

The compiler modifies this to create something like this before performing compilation:

```java
public class Outer {
   private int outerInt;

   public int access$000() {
      return outerInt;
   }

}


   class Inner$Outer {

   Outer outer;

   public void printOuterInt() {
      System.out.println("Outer int = " + outer.access$000());
   }
}
```

Although, logically, the inner class is part of the same code entity as the outer class it is compiled as a separate class. It, therefore, requires a synthetic bridge method to be created by the compiler to provide access to the private field of the outer class.

This JEP introduces the concept of nests, where two members of the same nest (Outer and Inner from our example) are nestmates. Two new attributes are defined for the class file format, NestHost and NestMembers. These changes are useful for other languages that support nested classes and are compiled to bytecodes.

This feature introduces three new methods to java.lang.Class:

- Class getNestHost()
- Class[] getNestMembers()
- boolean isNestmateOf(Class)

This feature also required changes to the Java Virtual Machine Specification (JVMS), specifically in section 5.4.4, Access Control.

JEP 309: Dynamic Class-File Constants

This JEP describes an extension to the class-file format to support a new constant-pool form, CONSTANT_Dynamic (often referred to in presentations as condy). The idea of a dynamic constant seems to be an oxymoron but, essentially, you can think of it like a final value in

Java. The constant-pool value is not set at compile-time (unlike the other constants) but uses a bootstrap method to determine the value at runtime. The value is therefore dynamic but, since its value is only set once, it is also constant.

This feature is primarily aimed at people developing new languages and compilers that will generate bytecodes and class files as output to be run on the JVM. It simplifies some of the tasks required for this.

This feature introduces a new class, java.lang.invoke.ConstantBootstraps, with nine new methods. I won't list them all here; these are the bootstrap methods for dynamically computed constants.

This feature required changes to the JVMS, specifically in the areas of how the invokespecial bytecode is used and section 4.4, The Constant Pool.

JEP 315: Improve Aarch64 Intrinsics

This was a JEP contributed by Red Hat. The JVM is now able to take advantage of more of the specialised instructions available in the Arm 64 instruction set. Specifically, this improves performance of the sin(), cos() and log() methods of the java.lang.Math class.

JEP 318: The Epsilon Garbage Collector

Red Hat also contributed this JEP. The Epsilon collector is somewhat unusual, in that it does not collect any garbage! It will allocate memory, as required, when new objects are instantiated but does not reclaim any space occupied by unreferenced objects.

When you first look at this, you think what is the point of that? It turns out that there are two uses:

1. Primarily, this collector is designed to enable new GC algorithms to be evaluated in terms of their performance impact. The idea is to run a sample application with the Epsilon GC and generate a set of metrics. The new GC algorithm is turned on, the same tests run and the metric results compared.
2. For very short-lived tasks (think serverless functions in the cloud) where you can guarantee that you will not exceed the memory allocated to the heap. This can improve performance by not having any overhead (including gathering statistics necessary to decide when to run the collector) on the application code.

If the heap space is exhausted, the JVM can be configured to fail in one of three ways:

1. A conventional OutOfMemoryError is thrown.
2. Perform a heap dump
3. Fail the JVM hard and optionally perform another task (like running a debugger).

JEP 324: Key Agreement with Curve25519 and Curve448

Cryptographic standards are continually changing and improving. In this case, the existing elliptic-curve Diffie-Hellman scheme is being replaced by Curve25519 and Curve448. This is the key agreement scheme defined by RFC-7748.

JEP 327: Unicode 10

The Java platform supports Unicode to enable all character sets to be processed. Since Unicode has been updated to version 10, the JDK has also been updated to support this revision to the standard.

I'm always intrigued to see what the Unicode maintainers find to include in new versions. Unicode 10 has 8,518 new symbols. This includes the Bitcoin symbol, the Nüshu character set (used by Chinese women to write poetry) as well as Soyombo and Zanabazar Square (which are characters used in historic Buddhist texts to write Sanskrit, Tibetan, and Mongolian). There are also lots more Emojis, including the long-awaited (apparently) Colbert Emoji.

Remember that since JDK 9, you can use UTF-8 in property files. This means any Unicode character can be used in a property file. Including Emojis. Or Nüshu.

JEP 328: Flight Recorder

Flight Recorder is a low-overhead data collection framework for the JVM. Prior to JDK 11, this was a commercial feature in the Oracle JDK binary. Now that Oracle is eliminating functional differences between the Oracle JDK and one built from OpenJDK source code, this feature has been contributed to the OpenJDK.

There are four parts to this:

- Provide APIs for producing and consuming data as events
- Provide a buffer mechanism and a binary data format
- Allow the configuration and filtering of events
- Provide events for the OS, the HotSpot JVM, and the JDK libraries

There are two new modules for this: jdk.jfr and jdk.management.jfr.

JEP 329: ChaCha20 and Poly1305 Cryptographic Algorithms

Similar to JEP 324, this is an updating of ciphers used by the JDK. In this case, implement the ChaCha20 and ChaCha20-Poly1305 ciphers as specified in RFC 7539. ChaCha20 is a relatively new stream cipher that can replace the older, insecure RC4 stream cipher.

JEP 331: Low-overhead Heap Profiling

Somewhat surprisingly, this is a JEP contributed by Google. This provides a way to get information about Java object heap allocations from the JVM that:

- Is low-overhead enough to be enabled by default continuously
- Is accessible via a well-defined, programmatic interface
- Can sample all allocations
- Can be defined in an implementation-independent way (i.e., not limited to a particular GC algorithm or VM implementation)
- Can give information about both live and dead Java objects.

JEP 332: Transport Layer Security (TLS) 1.3

TLS 1.3 (RFC 8446) is a major overhaul of the TLS protocol and provides significant security and performance improvements over previous versions. The JDK now supports this, although this does not extend to Datagram Transport Layer Security (DTLS).

JEP 333: ZGC A Scalable, Low Latency Garbage Collector

This is a new, experimental garbage collector designed for use with applications that require a large (multi-gigabyte) heap and low-latency. It uses a single generation heap (which is a bit unusual, given the accepted wisdom of the Weak Generational Hypothesis) and performs most (but not all) of the GC work concurrently with the application. It does this through the use of a read-barrier that intercepts each read to an object from the application and ensures that the reference returned is correct. This eliminates the issue of being able to relocate objects concurrently while application threads are running.

ZGC is region-based (like G1), NUMA aware and compacting. It is not intended as a general-purpose collector.

If you want a genuinely pauseless collector with low-latency, I can heartily recommend C4 in our Zing JVM.

JEP 335: Deprecate the Nashorn Scripting Engine

Nashorn was introduced in JDK 8 as a higher-performing replacement to the Rhino Javascript engine. The intention is to remove Nashorn, along with the associated APIs and jjs tool from a future version of Java. When this happens has not been decided yet. The possibility of using the Graal VM as a replacement has been suggested but how that will work has not been evaluated.

JEP 336: Deprecate the Pack200 Tools and APIs

Pack200 is a compression scheme for JAR files, introduced in Java SE 5.0. With the introduction of the JPMS in JDK 9, Pack200 is no longer used to compress the JDK itself. The pack200 and unpack200 tools, and the Pack200 API in java.util.jar are now deprecated and may be removed in a future version of the JDK. When this happens has not been specified.

With the recent changes to Oracle JDK distribution and support, there's been considerable uncertainty over the rights to use Oracle JDK vs Oracle's OpenJDK builds vs OpenJDK builds from other providers. There are also plans around free updates, and (new and existing) paid support models available from various vendors to consider. This document has a Shorter Version and a much Longer Version section with all of the detail.

Shorter Version

You can still get the Oracle JDK, Oracle's OpenJDK builds and OpenJDK by other providers for free (see the callout and the rest of the section for the nuances on this). This is possible because multiple providers offer implementations of the Java SE specification.

Java SE / OpenJDK / Oracle's OpenJDK Builds / Oracle JDK

*The **OpenJDK** community creates and maintains the (GPLv2+CE) open-source Reference Implementation (RI) of the **Java SE** Specification as governed by the Java Community Process (JCP) and defined through an umbrella Java Specification Request (JSR) for each feature release.*

*There are implementations of Java SE from various providers (such as Azul, Eclipse, IBM, Red Hat, Oracle, SAP, and others), the most common of these being **Oracle JDK**.*

***Oracle JDK 8** is undergoing the "End of Public Updates" process, which means there are no longer free updates for commercial use after January 2019. However, since Java SE 9, Oracle is also providing **Oracle's OpenJDK builds** which are free for commercial use, and there are free **OpenJDK** builds from other providers like AdoptOpenJDK, Azul, IBM, Red Hat, Linux distros et al. Providers prove that their implementation meets all the requirements of the Java SE specification by having it pass all the tests of the relevant Technology Compatibility Kit (TCK).*

Going forward there are several options to get a JDK. We focus on Java SE 8 (which is going through the end of public updates process as with earlier versions), and Java SE 11 which is the first Long Term Support (LTS) release under the new release cadence.

Staying with Java SE 8

Some people want to continue using Java SE 8 for various reasons.

1. Oracle will provide public updates of Oracle JDK 8 through at least December 2020 for personal desktop use and January 2019 for commercial use. After that, users can either go onto a paid support plan or use a Java SE 8 / OpenJDK 8 binary distribution from another provider.

2. You can continue to use Oracle JDK 8 indefinitely *without updates*.

3. If you are **not** using Oracle JDK 8, then your current Java SE 8 / OpenJDK 8 provider will provide updates and/or paid support plans to choose from.

I WANT $FREE AND FREE (AS IN USE) JAVA SE 8, WHAT DO I CHOOSE?

If you want updates of Java SE 8 after January 2019, use an OpenJDK binary distribution from an OpenJDK provider, i.e. Linux distros, [AdoptOpenJDK](), [Azul](), [IBM](), [Red Hat](), and others.

Getting Java SE 11 (LTS)

You have several options to choose from. Please read them carefully, especially as Oracle JDK is changing from Java SE 11 onwards.

[Starting with Java SE 11, Oracle provides their (OpenJDK based) JDK]() via

1. *Oracle OpenJDK builds*—Under the existing Open Source GPLv2+CE license, and

2. *Oracle JDK*—Under a paid commercial license (but free for development use), for those who do not wish to use the GPLv2+CE, or who are using an Oracle JDK with an Oracle product or service.

NOTE: Oracle plans to provide updates for its *Oracle OpenJDK builds* for two quarterly updates and then [transition users to the next version](), every six months (this includes LTS versions).

You can also get Java SE / OpenJDK binary distributions from a variety of other providers including Linux distros, AdoptOpenJDK, Azul, IBM, Oracle, Red Hat, and others. This includes updates for a variable length of time depending on whether it's an LTS version or not.

I WANT $FREE AND FREE (AS IN USE) JAVA SE 11+, WHAT DO I CHOOSE?

Use the Oracle OpenJDK build under the Open Source (GPLv2+CE) license and follow the new six-month release cadence **OR**

Use an OpenJDK binary distribution from an alternative OpenJDK provider, i.e. Linux distros, AdoptOpenJDK, Azul, IBM, Red Hat, and others.

Paid Support

Oracle plans to provide full paid support for Oracle JDK 8 until at least 2025 and Oracle JDK 11 until at least 2026 (details). There is a wide range of paid support options for Java SE / OpenJDK 8 and 11 binaries from Azul, IBM, Red Hat, and others.

The Longer Version

This section deliberately has a lot of detail as there are nuances that need to be clearly explained. Please do yourself and your colleagues a favour by setting aside some proper time to read this in full. You'll thank yourself for it, seriously.

We'd also like to thank Simon Ritter, Stephen Colebourne, Hendrik Ebbers, Donald Smith, Jonas Konrad and many others for their earlier posts and permission to reuse their material.

Appendix I—Signatories, Thanks and References gives a full list of accreditation and folks who are signatories to this document.

Feedback is welcome!

Change Log

This document will be updated over time as new information comes to light or if there is a verified correction to some factual data. Please check back here for updates and/or follow our @Java_Champions Twitter handle.

Version—Date—Comments

1.0.0–17 Sept 2018 1000 UTC—Initial Public Release

Dissemination

The following sheet is tracking known dissemination of this document. Please update if you share this doc!

Introduction

With the recent changes to Oracle JDK distribution and support, there has been considerable uncertainty over the future of Java, over the software lifecycles, and over vendor-provided support. This document summarises the changes Oracle is making, and the options available for users of Java SE.
WHAT DO WE MEAN BY FREE?
In a nutshell, the word "free" has two distinct meanings in software:
*"**Free as in beer**" refers to the cost (i.e. money) of the software (aka **$free**).*
*"**Free as in speech**" refers to what you are allowed to do with the software.*

*As explained in the Shorter Version, you can still get Java SE binaries **"free as in beer"** from Oracle and other Java SE / OpenJDK providers.*
*Although there are proprietary and/or restricted usage implementations of Java SE out there (Azul's Zing, Oracle's JDK etc), for a vast majority of users there is always the option of using an OpenJDK binary, which is **"free as in speech"** as it is GPLv2+CE licensed.*

These changes have happened within a short time frame creating a perfect storm of uncertainty as day to day developers, who don't follow the industry news closely, get caught up. This leads to factually incorrect posts like:

- DZone Article — Is Java in Jeopardy?

Which are luckily counterbalanced by more accurate posts such as:

- Donald Smith (Senior Director, Java Platform Product Management — Oracle) — Update and FAQ on the Java SE Release Cadence

- Simon Ritter (Deputy CTO — Azul) — Eliminating Java Update Confusion

- Stephen Colebourne (Joda-Time author) — Java is still available at Zero Cost and Java Options

- Hendrik Ebbers (Co-founder Karakun) — Do I need to pay for Java now?

This article will cover the main areas of concern and what's being done about those concerns by the ecosystem. By the end of this post, you should be reassured that Java SE is still being well looked after and that it has a future stronger than ever!

The New Six Month Release Cadence and LTS

Java SE now has a feature release every six months, using a new versioning scheme which was previously announced in 2017. Thanks to improvements in JCP processes, OpenJDK committers can now introduce spec changing features (such as var in Java SE 10) on the six-month cadence.

WHAT DOES LTS MEAN WITH REGARDS TO JAVA / OPENJDK?

Long Term Support (LTS) in OpenJDK is really just an understanding between the various contributors (led by Oracle) that the code line for Java SE 11 / 17 / 23 etc will be maintained for a longer period of time than six months.

Oracle will lead the first six months of an OpenJDK LTS code line, providing updates and producing Oracle OpenJDK builds, but will then afterward only provide updates for Oracle JDK, under a paid support plan.

However, Oracle will work with other OpenJDK vendors to hand over the OpenJDK LTS code line and allow them to continue working on it together to provide updates. Each vendor then has the choice of providing updates and/or paid support for the binaries they produce.

NOTE: *This does mean that Oracle's JDK could differ from the OpenJDK based binaries produced by other providers (this has always been the case). That said, as long as the binaries pass the TCK, you're assured that those binaries are compatible with the Java SE standard.*

Understanding the new versioning scheme (including what LTS means) and how new features are introduced impacts how each version is maintained. By maintenance, we mean the provision of update releases with security patches and important bug fixes.

UPDATES vs SUPPORT

Updates refer to the code patches that have gone into OpenJDK and Oracle JDK. These have typically gone in for

free, until vendors decide that there's an End of Public Updates *process*.
Support *means a commitment to fix bugs and it requires staff to answer users' problems, and that costs money. To be clear there has* never *been free support for Oracle JDK or OpenJDK.*

Up to and including OpenJDK 8 / Oracle JDK 8, updates were provided by Oracle and other OpenJDK committers **within** a *"feature release"*. Feature releases, such as 8u91, 8u111 and 8u131 (on a six-month cadence) were superseded by each subsequent feature release. For example, once 8u111 was released, you would not get updates on 8u91.

Starting with OpenJDK 9 / Oracle JDK 9, the new six-monthly release cycle came into effect and updates now occur **between** *"feature releases"*, i.e. Similar to 8u91 -> 8u111, once 12 is released, you will not get updates to 11 by Oracle (However, other OpenJDK committers, likely lead by Red Hat, will provide these).

Oracle Updates Plan

Until Java 8, Oracle provided updates for the Oracle JDK for a 3+ year lifecycle, and usage was permitted in personal as well as commercial settings. The updates provided no support, and support required the purchase of explicit licenses from Oracle. Paid support also entailed longer update cycles.

Starting with Java 9, Oracle has moved to a faster cadence for Oracle JDK and also started producing Oracle OpenJDK builds. Updates will generally be provided for 6 months before they are stopped upon release of the next version. If updates/support are required for a longer duration, or for production use, then it must be purchased from Oracle (i.e. You must be on Oracle JDK). Periodically, releases will be marked "LTS". These releases will be supported by Oracle through their standard support licenses for an extended period. As of right now, the Oracle update plan for Oracle OpenJDK builds, with updates, is as follows:

Oracle OpenJDK Build Version	Release date	Free updates superseded / ended (by Oracle)
8	March 2014	At least through January 2020 (personal desktop Ends January 2019 for commercial use
9	Sept 2017	Superseded by Oracle OpenJDK build 10
10	March 2018	To be superseded by Oracle OpenJDK build 11 in
11	Sept 2018	To be superseded by Oracle OpenJDK build 12 ir (this may be extended).
12	March 2019	To be superseded by Oracle OpenJDK build 13
13	Sept 2019	To be superseded by Oracle OpenJDK build 14

Oracle Updates Plan

The idea here is simple. As has been the model of Java SE going way back to the Sun era, Oracle focuses on new innovations and moving Java SE forward. Organizations who wish to remain on legacy versions can do so via commercial support offerings. Of course, for some Java SE users and development shops, such rapid upgrade is not feasible.

OpenJDK Updates Plan

The OpenJDK community works on a free, open-source implementation of the Java SE standard. Oracle contributes heavily to the project, and it is the basis for both Oracle OpenJDK builds and Oracle JDK. OpenJDK 11+ is interchangeable with Oracle JDK for applications that adhere to the Java SE standard and are using a build that has been tested against the TCK. Oracle will continue to contribute to OpenJDK while they provide updates for the corresponding Oracle OpenJDK build version. Once that version is superseded, Oracle will cease contributing to that version and start updating the next one.

Oracle has been highly receptive to the idea of community maintenance (for OpenJDK 6 and 7) and will continue to support handover of OpenJDK to the community to a qualified volunteering entity once they have moved on to working on the next version. Red Hat stepped in to globally lead (and provide regular updates to) OpenJDK 6 and OpenJDK 7 projects after Oracle ended updates for them. After Red Hat stopped updating OpenJDK 6, Azul Systems stepped in to lead the project and they continue to provide updates to this day.

Red Hat intends to apply for the leadership of OpenJDK 8 after Oracle stops updating it in January 2019. It is important to note that while Red Hat leads the OpenJDK 6 and 7 projects, they are not the sole contributors. Other vendors provide patches and fixes from time to time as well. With OpenJDK 8, there will be more contribution than ever before from non-Red Hat companies, such as Amazon, Azul, IBM, and others.

For consistency, the OpenJDK update cycle will be extended for the same versions that are deemed LTS for Oracle JDK. As of right now, OpenJDK support cycle is as follows:

NOTE: These times are subject to change and different providers all have slightly different timeline commitments. Therefore we use the term *"At Least"*.

Version	Release date	Free updates superseded / ended (by OpenJDK community members)
OpenJDK 6		Supported primarily by Azul systems
OpenJDK 7		At least through to June 2020 Supported primarily
OpenJDK 8 (LTS)	March 2014	At least through Sept 2023. Red Hat will apply to Jan 2019, and will be supported by Amazon, Azu IBM, and others.
OpenJDK 9	Sept 2017	Superseded by OpenJDK 10
OpenJDK 10	March 2018	To be superseded by OpenJDK 11 in Sept 2018
OpenJDK 11 (LTS)	Sept 2018	TBA, but comparable to the long OpenJDK 6 / 7 /
OpenJDK 12	March 2019	To be superseded by OpenJDK 13
OpenJDK 13	Sept 2019	To be superseded by OpenJDK 14

OpenJDK Updates Plan

Java SE / OpenJDK Providers

There are now a large number of Java SE / OpenJDK providers who provide either updates and/or paid support options. The following sections provide a lot of detail, if you prefer a shorter read then Stephen Colebourne's Java SE 11 Options post gives a summary.

UPDATES vs SUPPORT

Updates *refer to the code patches that have gone into OpenJDK and Oracle JDK. These have typically gone in for free, until vendors decide that there's an* End of Public Updates.

Support *means a commitment to fix bugs and it requires staff to answer users' problems, and that costs money. To be clear there has* never *been free support for Oracle JDK or OpenJDK.*

Why Would I Choose Commercial Support?

If you need a fix in a timely manner, someone to respond to your user requests, or if you want the reassurance that the binary you use is being backed by a vendor, then Azul, IBM, Red Hat, Oracle et al. all offer choices.

A PHILOSOPHICAL POINT ON PAYING FOR OPEN SOURCE SOFTWARE

The industry at large has settled firmly on Open Source Software as the way forward. Because of its "**Free as in speech**" nature, OSS licenses allow folks to modify and adapt other people's software without fear of punitive action.

Many folks also enjoy the "**Free as in beer**" nature of much OSS software, but this comes at a great cost to the authors! Software developers, like anyone else, need to put a roof over their heads and food on their table. Vendors like Oracle pour vast amounts of money into Java SE (think 10s of $ Millions per year at the very least) and they do need to somehow pay for that cost.

So although you're certainly not obliged to go with a paid support option with one of the vendors, sometimes it's worth thinking about how you, the end users, can support the Java SE ecosystem to ensure it has a long lasting future!

Provider Summary

Build yourself from Source

Build from Source [OpenJDK, no commercial support, need to self-build]:

- Mercurial: http://hg.openjdk.java.net/
- Tarballs (7+): https://openjdk-sources.osci.io/
- AdoptOpenJDK: https://www.github.com/AdoptOpenJDK/openjdk-build

Free Binary Distributions

Free Builds for Linux, Windows, Mac, etc. [OpenJDK, no commercial support]:

- AdoptOpenJDK (widest platform range)
- Azul Zulu
- Linux Distros
- Oracle OpenJDK builds—GPLv2+CE binary distribution
- SapMachine

Commercially Supported Distributions

Commercially supported [all Java SE compliant]:

Azul Systems [OpenJDK base]:

- Azul Java Product Support Roadmap
- Zulu and Zulu Enterprise Support Options

IBM [OpenJDK base classes + Eclipse OpenJ9 VM]:

- IBM Support For Runtimes

Oracle JDK [OpenJDK base]:

- Commercial Support for Java

Red Hat [OpenJDK base]:

- General Support information from Red Hat

Linux Distros

The various Linux distros will continue to provide OpenJDK for their respective distributions including but not limited to Debian, Ubuntu, CentOS, Fedora, Mint, Alpine et al.

- Linux Distros do not typically offer paid support (the exception being Red Hat for OpenJDK on RHEL).
- Please visit your distro homepage for more information.

AdoptOpenJDK

AdoptOpenJDK provides OpenJDK binary distributions (HotSpot and Eclipse OpenJ9) for a very wide range of platforms (Linux, Mac, Windows 32/64, Arm 32/64, z/OS, Solaris, AIX, PPC, s390 and more).

Support Options

- AdoptOpenJDK doesn't offer paid support. It simply provides well-tested binaries (some of which are TCK'd) from OpenJDK and Eclipse OpenJ9 upstream projects.
- IBM offers paid support for OpenJDK (with Eclipse OpenJ9 VM) binaries built at AdoptOpenJDK.

Important Links

- [AdoptOpenJDK](#) home page
- [AdoptOpenJDK Support Plans](#)

Azul

Azul provides OpenJDK binaries (Zulu) as well as a specialised Java platform (Zing).

Support Options

Azul offers an option for all companies that do not want to skip all Java SE versions between LTS releases but cannot switch to the newest version every 6 months. Next, to the support for all LTS releases, where Azul provides 1 more year of support than Oracle, Azul offers support for so-called Medium Term Support (MTS) releases for their Zulu JDK. Here you can buy commercial support for every second Java SE version regardless of if it is LTS or not. The support duration of these versions is different. Azul tries to provide a good time range to prepare a migration to the next version and defines 3 different durations for support of Java SE versions.

Unlike Oracle, the commercial support of Zulu is not defined per CPU but based on the number of systems. A system is defined as a physical or virtual server. The only difference between standard and premium support is the availability of the support. By buying premium support you can call Azul 24x7.

Important Links

- [Azul Java Product Support Roadmap](#)
- [Zulu and Zulu Enterprise Support Options](#).

IBM

IBM provides native JDK bundles for AIX, Linux (on x86, Power, zSystems), z/OS and IBM i. IBM offers the IBM SDK for Java SE versions for use with IBM products or platforms and for developer use from [developerWorks](). IBM also provides OpenJDK (with Eclipse OpenJ9) binaries built and tested at AdoptOpenJDK.

Support Options

For Java SE 7 and 8, IBM still provides security updates and bug fixes. The [IBM support lifecycle]() will continue to be updated. Based on the new Java SE release schedule IBM has announced that the non-LTS releases will be available as OpenJDK with OpenJ9 binaries from AdoptOpenJDK.

Important Links

- [Eclipse OpenJ9]()
- [AdoptOpenJDK OpenJ9 Binaries]()
- [IBM Support For Runtimes]()
- [IBM JDK Details]()

Oracle

Oracle now produces two JDK binaries: the traditional [Oracle JDK]() and an [Oracle OpenJDK build]().

Support Options

In June 2018, Oracle replaced its legacy *"Java SE Advanced"* perpetual license support product with a

Subscription based offering that includes license and support. One of them targets Java SE on the desktop and the other one Java SE on the server, cloud, and Java SE in general. If you do not use Java SE on the desktop the *"Java SE Subscription"* will be the right support model for you. If you use Java SE on the desktop for client applications the *"Java SE Desktop Subscription"* product is available. If your software uses a Java SE server and Java SE based clients you can subscribe to both offerings.

Commercial support for Java SE applications on the desktop might become quite important for some companies since Oracle will drop several important desktop features from the JDK starting with Java SE version 11. If you are using Java SE on the desktop we highly recommend to read the following articles:

- JavaFX Separate Module
- JavaFX Separate Module Part II
- JavaFX Separate Module Is Now Available
- Java client roadmap that was announced by Oracle in 2018.

Important Links

- Commercial Support for Java
- Published price list for "Java SE Subscription"

Red Hat

Red Hat produces OpenJDK binaries for various platforms that Red Hat Enterprise Linux runs on.

Support Options

Red Hat won't provide Java SE 9 and 10 releases. The next distribution that Red Hat plans to release is OpenJDK 11 for Red Hat Enterprise Linux 7. Currently, Java SE 8 is the supported release for Red Hat Enterprise Linux and the company will support it until 2023.

Important Links

- General Support information from Red Hat
- Unsupported community built binaries Linux/Windows from Red Hat upstream (ojdkbuild)

Java Desktop / Java Web Start / JavaFX

There are a number of changes with Desktop Java SE starting with Oracle JDK 11 that you need to be aware of.

JavaFX / OpenJFX

Starting with Java SE 11, neither the OpenJDK builds or the Oracle JDK binaries include the JavaFX libraries. The JavaFX components will now be delivered as a separate SDK, or as artifacts that can be used via build tools (e.g. Apache Maven, Gradle et al.). As a positive consequence of this decoupling, JavaFX development can now have its own roadmap.

JavaFX is still being developed in OpenJFX, which is a project under the OpenJDK community umbrella. Oracle, other companies and individuals in the wider community are actively developing JavaFX. An automatically synced GitHub mirror is created as well, lowering the barrier for developers to contribute code and issues to JavaFX.

At the moment builds for OpenJFX are only provided by Gluon. As all the OpenJFX source code is 100% open, others can create or distribute binaries as well. At OpenJFX, a similar approach as the one in OpenJDK is followed, where after releasing JavaFX 11, the focus is on JavaFX 12 and so on. JavaFX developers and users are encouraged to use the latest released version of OpenJFX.

Gluon provides a Support Plan for companies who want Long Term Support for JavaFX 11.

Java Packager

The javapackager, which allows bundling applications and its dependencies with (a subset of) the JVM is no longer part of OpenJFX and is removed from Oracle's JDK and Oracle OpenJDK builds starting with Java 11. A JEP has been submitted for adding a Java Packaging Tool to OpenJDK. While the new Java Packaging Tool will not be ready for the Java 11 release, Gluon is working on a tool allowing Java 11 applications to be packaged into native images.

Java WebStart

If you are using Java Web Start technology to distribute desktop clients you should take care about the current situation as fast as possible since Oracle has removed Web Start from Java.

- IcedTea-Web is an alternative you can use
- IBM will be supporting OpenJDK with OpenJ9 binaries with IcedTea-Web
- Community builds from Red Hat include a simplified IcedTea-Web installer (ojdkbuilds)
- Karakun is working on an OSS replacement for Web Start as well

FAQ

We recognize that the post above may not have the information explained in a manner which answers your exact question. So we have a FAQ.

OpenJDK variants vs each other and vs Oracle JDK

Q. Differences between OpenJDK vs Oracle's OpenJDK builds vs Oracle JDK?

We'll just talk about Java 11+ LTS releases here. Oracle JDK and Oracle OpenJDK builds are identical, but are licensed in different ways (commercial and GPLv2+CE respectively).

Oracle JDK / Oracle OpenJDK builds and OpenJDK builds from other providers will be built from the same source for the first six months of updates and should be interchangeable for that period. After six months Oracle JDK / Oracle OpenJDK builds will be built from Oracle's own fork. Other OpenJDK providers will continue to create binaries from the OpenJDK updates project. Oracle JDK / Oracle OpenJDK and OpenJDK builds from the other providers may therefore differ in small ways. Binaries from various parties may, of course, vary over time.

Q. Differences between OpenJDK from (non-Oracle) provider A vs provider B?

We'll just talk about LTS releases here. As has been the case with the Java SE 6 and Java SE 7 updates projects, various providers work together upstream in the OpenJDK community, which provides the common repositories, mailing lists, and other infra to share the work. This means the difference between OpenJDK-based binaries are mostly non-core features, like extended monitoring and diagnostic support. Although there may be small differences in the final binaries (perhaps a provider-specific tool etc) they will all at least have the same security and stability baseline as has been true for many years.

Oracle JDK / OpenJDK 8, 11 End of Public Updates by Oracle

With the Oracle JDK 8 and 11 End of Public Updates for Oracle happening soon, some folks are unclear on the ramifications:

Q. If I stay on Oracle JDK 8 / 11, do I have to pay to get security and bug fixes?

For Oracle JDK 8, for personal desktop use, then no. For commercial use after January 2019, then yes. For Oracle OpenJDK builds starting with Java SE 11, after the initial 6 months of updates, then yes.

Q. If I stay on OpenJDK 8 / 11, do I have to pay to get security and bug fixes?

Not necessarily. As was the case with Java SE 6 and Java SE 7, Oracle works with the OpenJDK community to transition the leadership of OpenJDK update projects to other contributors. This has worked well for over a decade. It is very likely Red Hat will continue this leadership in OpenJDK 8 and OpenJDK 11 updates with help from Oracle and other parties. This means important patches will get selectively backported. You then have the choice of taking downstream OpenJDK based binaries from a variety of providers for free, or as part of a paid support offering. In particular, there is an OpenJDK Vulnerability group which deals with 0-day exploits and CVE's and ensures that fixes get out as quickly as possible.

Q. Will Oracle's JDK 8 and 11 still be available for download (last public release)? For example, a

company has software that only runs on Oracle's JDK 8 and they provision a new machine after January 2019?

You can still download older versions of the Oracle JDK up to the point where the public updates stop. There is no reason to expect these archives to be removed. Moreover, Oracle JDK 8 continues to be free for personal desktop use through at least 2020.

Q. If someone is using Oracle JDK 8 to run commercial software, after January 2019 do they need to purchase a license?

No. The user can continue to use Oracle JDK 8 indefinitely without paying. The only cost is if they want to get updates beyond Jan 2019, in which case they will need to purchase an *"Oracle Java SE subscription"*. This follows the usual *"End of Public Updates"* process which has been in practice for well over a decade. Also, note that Oracle JDK 8 continues to be free for personal desktop use through at least 2020.

Q. What happens to Oracle Java Web Start after January 2019? Does it continue to run or at what point do you need to purchase a license?

Since Web Start is part of Oracle JDK 8 it will continue to work and can be used indefinitely without cost. As above if you need updates (bug fix and security patches) you will need to purchase a *"Java SE subscription"*. If your end users are consumers, they are covered for free until at least 2020 as Oracle JDK 8 will continue to be free for personal desktop use until at least the end of 2020. Oracle has stated that they will continue to support (i.e. provide commercial updates for) Java Web Start at least until March 2025.

Conclusion:

Java is a powerful programming language that became more interesting with its latest versions
As we saw it's going through a deep restructuration to be more involved in the proprietary world following the bill gates strategy on its languages keeping hands on the open source world to finally converge with each others.

Bibliography:

http://cr.openjdk.java.net/~iris/se/10/latestSpec

https://github.com/ReactiveX/RxJava/wiki/Backpressure

https://www.journaldev.com/

https://www.edureka.co/blog/

https://jaxenter.com/

https://www.valuecoders.com/blog/

https://www.azul.com/

https://medium.com/@javachampions/

Printed in Great Britain
by Amazon